"The Debt Lady" presents:

PAPER

OR

PLASTIC

The Debt Lady says:

Turn your American Dream

into <u>GREEN!</u>

A Guide to "Financial Health and
Prosperity"

Paper or Plastic

Copyright © 2012 by Jerri L. Simpson, Inc.

ISBN (978-1475291063)

To Cristal, Brandy and Cody,
my beautiful children,
for always believing in me and
letting me be exactly who I am.

Acknowledgments

J. Paul Getty once said,

"I'd rather have one percent of the efforts of 100 people than 100 percent of my own efforts."

If it wasn't for the diligence of all of the people in my life who assisted with this project, I would never have finished this book. "Paper or Plastic" has been a group effort from the start. And without my support group I wouldn't be writing my acknowledgements, but instead I'd be writing policies or articles and chatting on Facebook!

At the end of the day, it's not me who's the editor, illustrator, publicist, or any of the other hats that are worn on a project like this. It's the efforts of others that bring the whole thing together.

I'm not normally considered warm and fuzzy, but for this part of my book I'd like to get a little gushy with my appreciation of key people who have played vital roles in making this book a reality.

Felicia Baudar, one of my oldest and dearest friends has done all of the illustrations and a lot of the research for this book. We've been working together for almost 10 years in the financial industry and she has added a lot of the key ingredients to this book. Without her, the look and feel of this book would have been mediocre at best; she put in the pizzazz that I was looking for.

Vickie Jenkins helped with a major edit that needed to be done. After my first draft, let's just say that the book didn't flow from one topic to another; it was a mess. Vickie made it much easier on the eyes, and possible to understand what I was trying to say. Since she is an author herself, she was able to accomplish a smooth and easy transition between topics and chapters.

Marcy Brown has been doing the final edits of The Debt Lady newsletters and articles for years, and now the first book. She's always left my crazy attitude intact in all of my writings. Without her persistence in helping me in so many ways, this book would never have been completed—or for that matter, never even started! Marcy is a true friend and expert at what she does, I'm lucky to have her on my team.

Grateful acknowledgment is also made to the L. Ron Hubbard library. Without the knowledge I obtained from his works, this book would not of been possible.

The other people who have contributed to this book are clients, debtors, employees, acquaintances, consumers, business owners, celebrities, millionaires, beauticians, plumbers, lawyers, teachers, students, bookkeepers, babysitters, jewelry designers, cake decorators, creditors, accountants, dog trainers, nannies, makeup artists, massage therapists, auto mechanics, stock brokers, bankers, construction workers, personal chefs, the unemployed, and homemakers. I have spoken to thousands of people throughout the years in the financial industry, and every single one of them has helped me along the way to develop this book.

Thank you all for your efforts and wisdom to make this project a reality.

Jerri Simpson

Table of Contents

<u>Introduction</u>

The Debt Lady says,

"Dream big and have a full life, otherwise your napkin might fall off your lap and get stepped on by a credit card company." It's so true, isn't it?

Hello there, we haven't met before so here we go. I'm The Debt Lady. There, now that that's out of the way we can focus on what's important about this book and why you should read it. But first a little bit about me, if you don't mind. I've been consulting people on money, collecting money from people, filing lawsuits against people for money, taking people's money out of their bank accounts, garnishing money out of people's paychecks, helping budget people's money, controlling multi-million dollar corporations' money, donating money, spending money, having money, saving money and making money for over 30 years. I do have experience with money, wouldn't you say?

This book is a gem because it gives you tools to better handle your finances and your life. But more importantly, it has a picture of a smoking Santa. That's right, at one time in history, even Santa smoked. What does that have to do with the American Dream and finances, you ask?

Well this book has a bit of history. Okay don't freak out. I can safely assume that getting a history lesson is probably not the reason you picked up this book. But trust me when I say you'll learn something about the history of credit cards and advertising. That's where the smoking Santa comes in--you don't want to miss that part of the book.

It also gives you useful tools that you can use to help achieve your dreams and goals, and ultimately improve your quality of life. There will be exercises and things to do, so warm up by doing a couple jumping jacks, and touch your toes three times so that your back doesn't go out.

Money is a problem to most people, don't you agree? I thought so. This book teaches you how to *take the problem out of money* so that you can make more money and reach for your dreams in the process. Would you like that? Great! Thousands of people helped me write this book because I've consulted with thousands of people over the years. One for one, they've all had money problems in one form or another. Whether rich or poor, it didn't seem to matter--money was a problem. What my book does is help alleviate that problem so you can focus on the bigger picture, the better picture: your dreams and making them come true. Come with me on this journey; you won't regret it.

CHAPTER 1

Your American Dream

What *is* the American Dream? I've been searching for the answer to that question for years. When I first started looking into *what the American Dream really was*, I honestly thought it was about having material objects--money, a nice car, a big house, and literally a white picket fence. The more I researched it, the more I realized that it wasn't even <u>close</u> to what I thought it was. I've talked to a lot of people who have their own ideas of what the American Dream is. What's yours?

Take a moment to answer that question for yourself. It could be those material things that you've "always wanted," or a dream that you've had of being someone or something since you were a child.

> **What's Your Definition of the American Dream?**

Your answer won't be graded, judged or invalidated--it's yours and yours alone. By the end of this book you may realize that your American Dream is completely different than what you originally thought it was, and that's okay too. You have the power to change your mind and to decide to be or do something else if you choose to. You're free to dream about anything that you want, and to be able to accomplish that dream. So be honest with yourself.

One of the key skills you'll learn in this book is how to handle your finances. What's the connection between finances and the American Dream? Well, first of all, you have to have money to live on this planet, so being able to effectively handle your finances will solve any problems that you have about money. And second of all, getting rid of those money problems will help you focus on making your dreams come true.

I've been dealing with people's finances in one form or another for over 30 years, and I've watched times change to the point where Americans have gotten deeper in debt than ever before. Most people I talk to about finances have no idea how to handle them; they're juggling their credit cards, loans, rent or mortgage payments, and the rest of their bills are just a blur to them. When I ask people what they spend their money on, besides those obvious bank loans, they simply shrug their shoulders and look confused. They can't answer the question because they honestly don't know how much they spend on basic expenses. They see no light at the end of that dark "debt tunnel" that they live in, and don't feel like they'll ever get out of it.

So if you want to make your American Dream more than just a *dream*, you have to learn how to handle money. For instance, if you dream of being an actor, you still have to make money, manage your money, and handle your debt, while at the same time building your acting skills, auditioning for parts, and working towards achieving that dream. The bottom line is, in order to survive, you need money. So, to reach your dreams you have to know how to manage your money. It's hard to follow a dream when you're worrying about money all the time—where it's coming from or whether there's enough to go around. Worrying takes up a lot of time and energy. Who needs that? Not me. I'd rather spend my time and energy on planning my future and reaching my goals.

I've put this book together for two reasons—to help people identify their dreams, and to give them tools to better understand money and finances in order to <u>achieve</u> those dreams. I'm not interested in telling you what to do or how to live your life. All I'm trying to do is give you a little bit of information so that you can decide for yourself how to live your life, and to help you live it without money problems.

You can change your destiny; you can change your life; you can be the person you want to be. <u>You</u> are in charge and <u>you</u> will be in control. I'm just supplying the tools. <u>You</u> have to decide to *DO* something about it, and then take the steps to make it happen. So let's start with one of the most common questions in this whole American Dream topic:

> **If I won the lottery or had all the money in the world, would I have my American Dream?**

Good question isn't it? When I've been in situations where I haven't had the money to pay a bill, or in some cases in the '80s, I couldn't put food on the table for my two kids, I've dreamed of winning the lottery. I guess in order to actually win the lottery I would have had to buy a ticket, and in those days, I didn't have the extra money to do that either. Times were tough and I lived paycheck to paycheck. If I wrote a check at the grocery store I could count on it not hitting my bank for a full week (compared to nowadays when you use your debit card or write a check, and the money comes out of your account the same day and in some cases, the instant they swipe it!). I took advantage of that when I didn't have food in the house. Hot dogs and macaroni and cheese were among our normal dinners, and the Salvation Army and Goodwill were where most of my kids' clothes came from. You could say that as a single parent, I was at the *LOW* end of the income spectrum. I was a bill collector at the time and worked on a small monthly salary of $780, plus commissions. My daycare bill alone was over $800 a month, so I *HAD* to make commissions. If I didn't, we wouldn't eat. I had to get very creative when I paid my bills. One year a co-worker surprised me with a Thanksgiving dinner because she knew I didn't have the money to pay for it. There was a box of food waiting for me when I got home from work on that Wednesday evening. If it wasn't for her, we would have had our normal hot dog dinner; at least I was planning on making turkey franks instead of beef.

That same year I talked to a man who'd won the lottery—he pocketed over a million dollars. But in less than a year he was flat broke and owed two million dollars. I asked him how that had happened, and he told me that because he suddenly had a lot of money he was offered more credit by the banks, and the more credit he was given the more he spent. After he got his lottery check he quit his job after being there for over 15 years. He told me that he regretted leaving because he'd loved his job.

He was planning on using some of his lottery winnings to pay off his debt, but other things presented themselves, like a 10 million dollar house requiring an enormous down payment. He told me that he lost the house after 18 months because he could no longer afford the payments. What surprised me most was when he told me that he didn't feel like he'd <u>earned</u> the money himself and felt weird about keeping it. So he spent it--<u>all of it</u>.

Was he happy? You would think so, at least for a short time, because he didn't have to worry about money. But the answer is—no. He was really only happy for about a minute and a half and in the end he was more stressed out than ever before.

Have you ever noticed that children sometimes break a new toy very quickly after they get it, or stop playing with it after a short period of time? Why is that? Well it turns out that even children like to <u>earn</u> things—that is, to *DO* things in exchange for money or rewards. When a child comes to you and wants to help with the dishes or take out the garbage, it's important that you <u>let them help you</u>. Why, you ask? Because they, too, want to work—to *DO* something in exchange for the money or items that you have provided for them. If you just give them anything they want and never let them *DO* anything for you in exchange, they will actually become resentful of you. All you've done is create a spoiled child. You know the type. They have no real understanding of the value of things because they've never actually had to work for them. And it only gets worse the older they get.

The lottery winner's life had been turned upside down. He ended up having <u>more</u> debt than he had before he'd won the lottery. And since he'd quit his job, he had no source of income to pay off all the debt he'd racked up. You may think that you would never do anything like that because you would be smarter about it, but until you actually come into a large amount of money, you don't know what you'd do. People act bizarre when money's involved. He didn't earn it and he blew it--it's as simple as that.

What if instead you <u>earned</u> money by producing a product that you <u>cared</u> about? And what if, as you earned that money for your good production, you were better trained on how to handle credit cards, debt, and the income and outflow of money, so that money wouldn't be such a worry in your life? You could actually focus on reaching your American Dream, and the odds of winning would be much better than in any lottery. Interested? **Read on.**

CHAPTER

<u>Recovering Your American Dream</u>

If you had trouble listing your idea of an American Dream in the first chapter, you're not alone. For many people, dreams are just that—<u>dreams</u>—and goals are long gone. But without dreams and goals, there's nothing to strive for. When you work day to day with no focus on what you actually want to <u>achieve</u>, it can leave you spinning around in circles and going nowhere.

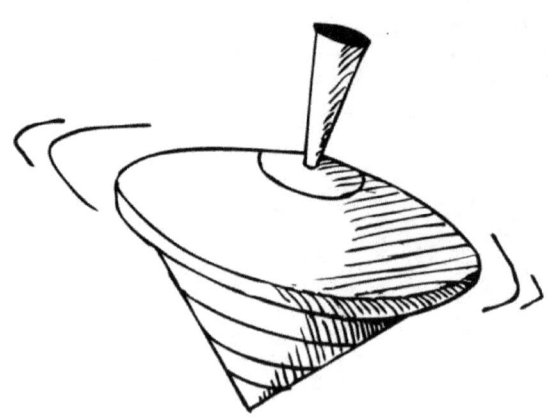

> **Why do people spend hours a day playing video games?**

It's because they don't have any fun games to play in life or at work. They feel they can't win any of the games of life and they certainly have no excitement on the job. So getting to the next level on a challenging video game is at least something they can win at and it's fun.

Those who bury themselves in hours of television shows or movies may feel the same lack of interest and excitement in their own lives. Lack of dreams and goals in life can also cause you to spend hours online or at the mall, shopping for _things_ to make you happy and putting those _things_ on your credit cards so that you _have_ a bunch of stuff. Even though you can't afford those _things_, the credit card company won't mind lending you the money so that their pockets get deeper. One day you could wake up and realize that you've stopped playing life's games altogether—and end up falling back asleep on the couch, or checking out altogether with alcohol or drugs. So, how do we pull ourselves out of Dullsville and get going on our dreams and goals? Let's start with tiny steps like, GET OFF THE COUCH.

If you just get up and complete one task, such as doing the dishes or your laundry, making your bed, mowing the lawn, or washing the car, you can start to get that feeling of getting something _accomplished_. Maybe you finish the last four pieces of that puzzle so it's finally complete. People get motivated by _producing something_. It's a good idea to start with small, around-the-house tasks that are within your control. Even if that means cleaning the kitchen so you can have shiny counters and a swept floor. It's the small things that can make all the difference in the world for your attitude and outlook on life.

Getting Motivated at Work

Some Americans go to work every day and hate it. Work shouldn't be a chore; it should be fun and exciting and you should get something out of it. If you're doing something you hate and are too afraid to quit and find another job, it's time to figure out a solution that will work, at least temporarily until you can start focusing on that American Dream. So, let's start with that "production" idea and how to make work as much of a game as those online toys or video games.

If you're one of the millions of Americans who are currently unemployed, this is the time to take stock of what you like to do or want to learn to do, and start creating your plan. Those around-the-house chores will help keep you producing while you look for work. Also, every time you send out a resume or make a call to check on a potential job, you are taking steps to produce your next product—which is YOU, as a skilled, positive, willing employee, consultant, or business owner. If the hunt for a specific job is taking too long, just get a job—<u>any</u> job—and start <u>producing</u>. You'll feel better.

If you're currently employed, take a look at your job and figure out exactly <u>what</u> your product is.

- **Do you finish the paperwork so the company's products can get out the door?**
- **Do you sell something?**
- **Are you part of a team that helps people become healthier or smarter?**
- **Do you manage a team of people who depend on you?**
- **Do you deliver pizzas?**

Everyone does something at work other than hang around the coffee pot and talk about last night's TV shows. Identify <u>your</u> product and start keeping statistics on it.

- **How many do you produce?**
- **How many passed inspection?**
- **How many calls did you make today?**

- How many trucks did you load?

- How many tips did you make?

Keep track of these every day, so that tomorrow you know what you need to accomplish to do more than the day before. Make a game out of it and play that game every day! Even if others don't care—YOU should. Remember, this is about you being able to handle work and income so that you can create YOUR American Dream. So, *get to work.*

If you have a job but it's an unacceptable work environment—where the best producers are not rewarded, or the people are hostile or unethical—keep your <u>own</u> integrity intact while you start shopping for a workplace that will appreciate what you produce.

If you used to like your job but have gotten tired or disillusioned with it, review the past years and your accomplishments. Write them down. What were the parts that you enjoyed? What took you away from that? Separating one from the other will help you focus on doing what you like, while you handle the other issues. Are you contributing to that tiredness or your bad attitude at work? For instance:

- Do you stay up too late playing video games?
- Do you take lunches that are a little too long?
- Do you drink during your lunch hour?
- Do you drink regularly and go to work with a hangover?
- Do you lie to your boss or co-workers?
- Do you do something else when you're supposed to be working?

- **Have you ever taken office supplies from the workplace and used them for your own personal use?**

If you're doing any of these things, then knock it off and get honest and change what you're doing. And for goodness sakes, take that stapler back to the office--it wasn't yours to take!

You'll be amazed at how just being honest and actually DOING the work will make you feel better. Do you actually like your job overall, but still find it dull, tiring, or exasperating? If so, look at what is NOT working, and change what is in your power to change.

You don't like your immediate supervisor? See if you can transfer to another department. You don't get lunch breaks or 15 minute breaks? Go online and get the law for your state and bring it up to your supervisor. The law is the law and you have to be allowed to take breaks and eat lunch. Do you get yelled at every day because you don't know how to do something? Find out how to do it and do it well!

The point is you should be productive and feel good about what you're doing, and know that you <u>are</u> contributing to the bottom line. You're not just falling asleep at work and waiting to get home so that you can beat the next level on that video game or catch up on your favorite TV shows. Then you'll stay productive enough to keep the money coming in while this book teaches you how to handle that money so you can achieve your American Dream.

What I'm saying is—if you haven't won the lottery, or don't have all of the money you want, what about going to that place where you make money and <u>get to it</u>? Do the job, fully and completely. Be proud of your work and what you do and be the person that you want to be. You'll be amazed at how satisfying it will be.

CHAPTER 3

American Dreams and Time Lines

So where did this "American Dream" concept come from anyway? Actually, it's been around for a long time and has so many definitions that it's hard to determine what the original intention of it really was.

I recently had someone survey me over the phone about the current economy. One of the questions she asked was, "Do you think that the problems with the economy will make it impossible to obtain the American Dream?" I asked her what <u>she</u> thought the American Dream was. She simply ignored my question and moved on to the rest of her survey.

When I hung up the phone I was so intrigued about this that I started talking to people and doing surveys of my own. I wanted to find out exactly how people defined the American Dream. Their responses broke down into three categories, based mostly upon age.

The first response came from a woman born in the 1930s: "The American dream is the ability to lead a peaceful life, free of government harassment. Every individual should be free to secure their life, liberty and the pursuit of happiness as was guaranteed in America's founding documents. It is not home ownership—that is a marketing concept pushed by the real estate industry."

While she was growing up, there wasn't as much advertising as there is today and the idea of the American dream was more about happiness and peace.

A man who was born in the 1950s responded: "The American dream means to me to feel happy, joyous and free. To know you can be accepted for who you are with respect and dignity, whatever your sex, religion, race, political or sexual preferences. To live without fear. To feel a part of, not separate from. To have the same resources available to learn and experience what you desire."

I have definitely noticed similarities among baby boomers. Their American Dream is more focused towards feeling happy and accepted.

The third response came from a 20-something girl who wrote: **"The American dream is a trap since it's constantly thrown at you how you should be, act or what you should own."**

As you can see, the differences in responses from decade to decade are like night and day. I continued to talk to people about this, and asked <u>where</u> they got their definition of this so-called "American Dream." Many told me that they never learned it from anywhere--they just assumed what it was, based on what other people said, or on things that they saw on television or in movies.

In some cases, people told me that they had an idea that the American Dream was kind of like hot dogs, baseball and Chevrolet. Sounds like a TV ad—for the American Ideal.

The "Stuff" Dreams are Made of

As I said, I've worked with people on and around the subject of money for more than 30 years, and I've seen it over and over—people fall on their faces trying to achieve their <u>financial</u> American Dream due to problems with debt. They seem to be stuck to the belief that the American Dream is about having more stuff, more money, a lot more credit and that perfect credit score. They dug a great big hole of debt and they can't get out.

I've found that most people have their attention on money most of the time. It seems to me that there is nothing that creates more problems than money.

I just couldn't believe that the American Dream had to do with money or having stuff, because I'd seen that dream turn into a nightmare for so many people. There <u>had</u> to be more to it.

My research led me to some interesting findings in this quest for the truth. I had to do some digging through history, questioning every type of concept—from a smoking Santa to our Founding Fathers—to find out <u>where</u> those definitions or misconceptions of the American Dream came from. I'm sharing my findings with you in this book. Then you can review the history and decide for yourself what you want to take from it to improve your own life. As you begin to create your <u>own</u> definition of the American Dream, this book will help you take the steps to make your dreams a reality.

Okay, you're probably still stuck on the last paragraph, thinking about that smoking Santa. I'll explain that bit of history in a minute. But first—let's look at how the world has been defining the "American Dream".

CHAPTER 4

The American Dream Defined

I went online to research definitions of the American Dream to see if I could find the information that I was looking for. I couldn't believe how many different definitions there were. The first one I looked at was from *Collins English Dictionary* which defined the American Dream as: ***"The notion that the American social, economic and political system makes SUCCESS possible for every individual."***

I wanted to know more about "success" so I looked at the *Free Dictionary Online*. One of the definitions of success is: ***"The achievement of something desired, planned, or attempted."***

What an excellent definition! It's about dreaming about or wanting something and getting it. If the American Dream is about success, then people who are successful have achieved the American Dream, right? I don't think so; I had to look further.

I checked the next definition in the *Merriam-Webster* dictionary and the example sentence was: *"With the acquisition of a BIG HOUSE IN THE SUBURBS, they felt as though the American dream had indeed become a reality for them."*

So it's about a big house in the suburbs and being successful. If that's the case, then why are so many Americans in foreclosure trouble and having problems making ends meet?

When I checked out some of the quotes from famous people, I came across Martin Luther King, Jr's speech that stated: *"I have a dream that one day this nation will rise up and live out the true meaning of its creed: we hold these truths to be self-evident, THAT ALL MEN ARE CREATED EQUAL."*

All right, fantastic, so we are all equal, we live in a big house in the suburbs and we are successful. So what exactly does that mean? Or better yet, how do we get it?

Arnold Schwarzenegger, the famous body builder turned movie star, turned Governor of California, turned, well you know the rest, once said: **"My fellow Americans, this is an amazing moment for me. To think that a once scrawny boy from Austria could grow up and become Governor of California and stand in Madison Square Garden to speak on behalf of the President of the United States that is AN IMMIGRANT'S DREAM. It is the American dream."**

Okay, so now we have it defined by a dude from another country who came to America, became Governor of a state where everyone is equal to everyone else and has a big house in the suburbs and is incredibly successful. Even though Arnold Schwarzenegger has had all of those things, look at the very awkward position that he put himself in during 2011, because of his earlier personal life decisions. Do you think that now he is really happy and has achieved that dream, or has he taken advantage of it by doing things that were unethical and not confessing until after he left office? Would the people of California have voted for him if they'd known what he'd done? What happened to THAT American Dream?

As I continued my search, I was less convinced, and more confused. I surveyed some other people and got the most random answers to the question. My favorite was from a 25-year-old single female who wrote her description of the American Dream: *"The big house with the white picket fence with the dogs and cats and a perfect husband that's tall dark and handsome and 2 to 3 beautiful kids. MAKING ENOUGH*

MONEY TO LIVE WITH NO WORRIES at all about finances for the entire family."

Okay, so let's summarize the American Dream, according to my research so far. It has to do with being from another country, living in a great big house, with a bunch of money, pets, a spouse and kids, being successful and equal to everyone else. Now, before I comment on that let's look at the definition of "equal" in *The Free Dictionary Online*. One of the definitions of equal is: *"Having the same privileges, status, or rights."*

We should all be able to have rights and that is probably the definition most people use when they talk about everyone being "equal." It makes sense to me that we all have the ability to do anything we want to do with no one stopping us. We want to have equal rights, but don't really want to be equal to our fellow man, because we're not all the same. And the last thing we want to do is to be compared to someone else because they do something better or have the best education.

Instead, think of it this way: I am exactly who I am and who I want to be; I am doing everything I can do and I love doing it. I have all of the opportunities that I need to do what it is that I want to do, and I will take advantage of those opportunities. Could you imagine that? Think about it. It's not about being like everybody else, but instead, it's about having the opportunity to have anything you want to have because you're who you want to be and are doing exactly what you want to do based on who you are. Interesting concept, right?

How can having a bunch of stuff be my American Dream? Well trust me when I say, IT ISN'T!

I am successful in what I do because it is what I want to do and what I make of it. It's not what anyone else thinks of me, but what I think of myself. I am successful to myself and for myself and therefore I am me.

Now as for the house and the money, again, we have to have the money so that restaurants don't kick us out because we're not wearing shoes, and we have to have the house for the purpose of shelter. Those things are important for survival, but they're just _things_. I know we need that stupid money to get by, but is it the American Dream? I'm going to let you answer that for yourself, AFTER you finish this book.

The Pursuit of Happiness

Finally I found the concept that made the most sense to me—in the Declaration of Independence. The Founding Fathers defined the American Dream when they wrote: _**"We hold these truths to be self-evident, that all men are created equal, that they are endowed by their Creator with certain unalienable Rights that among these are Life, Liberty and the pursuit of Happiness."**_

Yes, Martin Luther King, Jr. focused on the "equality" segment of that document. But now let's look at the rest of it. If you break the statement down, you find that Life means we are living; we are BEING someone or something. Liberty means freedom--we are free to dream up whatever we want. The Pursuit of Happiness means to get out and *DO* what we want in order to HAVE that dream.

You see the <u>order</u> of that statement? BE something first—infuse yourself with Life, then *DO* the activities that will bring the things for you to *HAVE*.

For example—if you want as your goal to *HAVE* a successful acting career, you must first *BE* an actor, that is, assume that identity. It means you're not a fan, or a TV or movie viewer, watching actors. You are *BEING* an actor. Then, *DO* the things that will bring you that acting career—take acting classes, have headshots made, get current lists of casting directors, and contact people daily to let them know that you are an actor, in pursuit of the career, the job, the TV commercial, etc. Got it?

BE, DO, then *HAVE*, in that order. You don't have to have a lot of money to do these things. Some people think that in order to *DO* what they want to do they need money. Never let that stop you from doing what you want to do based on your dreams. You can do a lot of research on the internet. Put communication out on Facebook and other social media websites and network in other ways. Tell people what you're doing. You're an actor. If you need to take acting classes, find out about scholarships, or go to colleges or your community center to see if they have free seminars. Go to local old folk's homes, hospitals or daycare centers and ask to perform. Put together a show with your other actor friends and *DO* it. Or put your own acting class together with people you know and *BE* that actor and *DO* those things that you need to do to *BE* who and what you want to be. By doing these things, you will have what you want to have, you will get that part because you are *BEING* and *DOING* what you need to do to *HAVE* what you want--an acting career.

Why have so many American Dreams failed? Because people thought they had to *HAVE* first. Have the nice car, the expensive vacation, the big-screen TV or the part in that new reality TV show. If you put the *HAVE* first, it's all backwards. You're not *DOING* what it takes to create that goal, and you're not *BEING* the identity of what you want. So in order to *HAVE* that acting career you must first *BE* and *DO*.

Life, liberty and the pursuit of happiness--no wonder it's called the Declaration of Independence! You're free to make your dreams come true! This is why people came to this country in the first place, and why people continue to arrive here, for that freedom to *BE, DO* and *HAVE*.

There was one other interesting definition I uncovered, which gave me a new reason to continue working on this book. I found it in the *Cultural Dictionary*, which stated that the American Dream includes: **"Hope for prosperity and happiness, symbolized particularly by having a house of one's own. Possibly applied at first to the hopes of immigrants, the phrase now applies to all except the very rich and suggests *a confident hope that one's children's economic and social condition will be better than one's own.*"**

This is an interesting definition because it implies that now we are looking at our children's futures as well as our own. To me that means that if we do NOW what needs to be done to handle our own lives, then our kids will be able to follow our example and make a great life for themselves based on decisions that they make on their own, not on what they are told to do. If we just sit around in hopes that someday our kids will have it better than we do, then we are showing them that something could possibly happen in the future, yet we are doing nothing about it now to accomplish it. Children, whether we like it or not, make decisions based upon their parents' examples. So if we are who we really want to *BE* and we *DO* everything we can do to improve our lives, then we'll show them that they, too, can do it. And not by waiting around in hopes that one day a politician will knock on the door and hand out thousands of dollars, a house in the suburbs and that white picket fence that everybody seems to have to have before they obtain their ultimate goals in life, their American Dream.

I don't know about you but I'm not going to sit around waiting for something that I know will never happen. I will do something about it now, today, this minute and I will set that example so that my kids will be who they want to be, while they're active and producing and going for what they want.

This is the American Dream that I've been looking for-- Life, liberty, and the pursuit of happiness. It's about being who you truly are, and having the opportunity and freedom to work towards that dream by doing what's necessary to get there. Even if it's being the local garbage collector because that's exactly who you WANT to BE, you do it proudly and happily and have everything in life that you want. You're *BEING* and *DOING* and therefore *HAVE* your life the way YOU want it!

For a long time, people have felt and have been told that they have to *HAVE* without doing the other two—and they fail at it. They can't have things unless they buy them but they can't buy them without having money. So by following this simple rule of *BE* before you *DO*, and *DO* before you *HAVE*, you will obtain your American Dream. And your children will be free to achieve theirs as well.

Needs vs. Wants

Speaking of children—let's look at how our daily activities help create specific versions of the American Dream. When was the last time you had that discussion with your son or daughter about what they "absolutely HAD to have" in order to fit in with other kids? What we "need" versus what we "want" (disguised as "have to have") blurs in those debates around the kitchen table or at the mall.

We have to have food. Without it I'm afraid our bodies would malfunction and die. They make us pay for food at the store these days instead of growing it in our backyards like we used to.

We have to have clothing, because if we're not dressed, people look at us funny or kick us out of their restaurants. Most of us don't make our own clothes anymore. I don't know about you but I got a "D" in sewing in the 7th grade and can barely stitch on a button. We go to the mall for the latest and greatest fashion (yes I'm guilty of this too).

Of course we have to have a roof over our heads. I would prefer staring at the stars at night before I go to sleep, but the contractor who built my house decided that it would sell for more money with a roof on it. We don't live in grass huts that we made with our bare hands.

We have to have shoes, because most places insist on it and tell us so with their intimidating sign stating, "No Shoes, No Shirt, No Service."

We could wear animal skins on our feet from that animal that we killed for dinner last night, but I haven't seen a deer walking down my street lately and those coyotes and raccoons that do, don't look too appetizing.

Now that we've moved out of the caveman days and have secured our basic needs of food, shelter, etc., the technological world tugs at our arm, telling us our "needs" and "wants" have changed.

We are told that without our computers, cell phones, and the rest of the electronic age products, we can't communicate; and that we absolutely need them. But is that really correct? Do we know how to communicate without all of those things? There were none of those when I was growing up and I communicated to people, in person, every single day. Imagine it! I liked the fact that my mother couldn't reach me any time she wanted to and I was free to do what I wanted to do without feeling like I was on an electronic leash. I know that times have changed, but there is a point when we should let kids be kids and not let them have phones when they're six years old. Those kids will grow up knowing how to text and talk on the phone, but having a real, face-to-face conversation with their parents will be extinct.

I've been guilty of this non-communication issue. One day I was playing "Words with Friends" on my phone against my son and daughter who were sitting in the same room with me watching TV. We were basically staring at the TV while playing a game on our phones and not communicating with each other at all, unless it meant asking the other to hurry up and play so that we could make our move.

I went to the Olive Garden a few months ago and there were four couples waiting to be seated. I saw that all eight of them were on their phones. It was quite amazing to watch; they were all hunched over in their seats, not talking to each other or even talking on the phone, but rather texting or playing games instead. The only time they moved or said anything was to stand up and be seated. The electronic leash has created other effects on people's bodies. I'm not even going to get into the brain tumors that are being caused by cell phones, because that would be a book in itself. The other day my chiropractor told me that she's been seeing more and more people with hernias of the stomach. I asked her for her theory on what was causing the problem. She explained to me that too many people are sitting hunched over their computers for long stretches of time, and their stomachs are being pushed up under their ribcage, which is causing problems with digestion and the stomach in general.

Yikes! Our lives revolve around the latest and greatest technology, right? Well with some people that's absolutely true. But do we have to have these things to survive? No, we don't. But they sure make life convenient, don't they? So how did these "wants" get turned into "needs" in the first place? Who convinced us that we HAD TO HAVE stuff?

CHAPTER 5

The Lie

Let's take a look at the real lie in this whole American Dream thing. The lie is really about all those things that we're "supposed" to have, because we're told that we have to have them in order to be what they think we should be, not what we want to be ourselves.

Don't believe me? Run this test yourself: Hit the mute button on the TV and write down the impressions you get of each commercial--not the words, but just the emotional impressions. What is each ad selling you? Happiness is a better phone! You get the ultra-hip beautiful girl or handsome guy if you wear the right brand of jeans! That truck takes you to all the best places in the world! If you look at that picture on TV and think, "I'm not that. But I want to be like that. If I have that, then I'll be happy," THEY'VE HOOKED YOU.

> The lie is that you are who everybody <u>else</u> says you are or who you should be, and could be, <u>IF</u> you bought all of their stuff.

The TRUTH is—you are an amazing person! You are unique, just the way you are right now. You comb your hair a certain way. You laugh a certain way. You are YOU. So are you lying to yourself by trying to be somebody that you're not? If so, how did that start? Well, there are more than just TV ads behind the manufacturing of the lie.

Have you ever been told that you had to be a certain way or do a certain thing—something that you weren't and didn't want to be or do? Let me give you an example here with parents. Were you ever told that you should be a baseball player or a ballerina when you were little, and you agreed only because your parents wanted you to, or worse yet, because they <u>made</u> you? Did your parents want you to marry so-and-so, or to be "just like Dad" and become a construction worker?

> **Were you told that you were**
>
> **fat or ugly or stupid or clumsy?**

It wasn't your own opinion of yourself, but someone else's. And then you agreed. Did you feel like you were losing control of yourself or your life at that point? Be honest with yourself when you answer that question.

Whatever your answer, I totally understand, because that is exactly the way it was with me when I was little. I believed what I was told—that I was fat and ugly—and when I looked in the mirror that's what I saw. In a lot of these cases we are told something, and instead of kicking it back to the person and saying, "NO I'M NOT" we tend to agree with the person because of who they are, or because of the respect we have for them. We believe them and we become that thing. It doesn't matter if it's a family member, a fireman, your best friend, a spouse, a co-worker, a neighbor, or a teacher who is doing the labeling; we can agree so strongly with someone else that it makes us that label.

What about your boss telling you to do a job that you weren't trained to do? You fumble around, get confused and go home and kick the dog because the job wasn't something you wanted to do or were trained to do. You didn't say anything to your boss at the time; you just tried to do it and failed. Does that make you a failure? Sometimes we feel that way about ourselves, when all that should have happened was to tell the boss that you didn't know how to do the job, and if you got trained you'd be able to do it. It's so much simpler to have that agreement and understanding so that you don't have to invent excuses. You handle it then and there with communication.

> **The lie is that you have to live your life the way somebody else tells you to live it.**

Let's take another example—the influence that comes from a psychiatrist or medical doctor. They sit across from you in their office and tell you that you have Leaky Eye Syndrome, Twitchy Leg Syndrome, ADHD, Bi-polar Disorder, or Excessive Internet Syndrome. Then they tell you that your insurance company will pay for the drug that you should take to handle your "disorder." They say it's something you have to live with, but that with medication, you can "manage" your disease.

What's happening is that the doctor is trying to tell you what or who you are.   Let's say you've just been diagnosed with ADHD. You have to take these drugs and go to therapy every week and now "it" is what you have. And "it" becomes your IDENTITY.

Before you know it, you're saying, "I have ADHD," or, "I'm obsessive-compulsive." Really? Is that who you really are? You, in this case, made no decisions on your own. You were told exactly what you were. That put you in a position where you were no longer in control of your own life, but were being controlled by doctors who have no business telling you what or who you are, because there is no proof that any of those "disorders" actually exist in the first place.

In actuality you're not making up your own mind about who you *ARE*, what you're *DOING* with your life, or what you *HAVE*. What you're doing is accepting a "diagnosis" from someone who doesn't know what they're talking about (but they'll recite a lot of statistics to try to convince you how "true" it is and how bad off you are).

Have you found that after you started taking pills for some "disorder or condition," you actually felt worse, not better? And did the doctor give you more pills to counteract the side effects of the first drug? Or perhaps they told you that the drugs only work "in combination with other drugs?"

Psychiatrists are drugging children under five years old because they don't sit still, calling that habit a "mental disorder." Why should a five-year-old sit still? They have lots of energy! So you, as a parent, listen to this doctor who says your child has a "mental disorder," or he says you have a "mental disorder." And now you or your child are labeled as something that you didn't agree to. You're being told you're something you never decided to *BE*. That IS the biggest lie of all—that you are that *thing*. The next time a doctor or psychiatrist diagnoses you with anything, ask to see the PROOF. Not the opinion, but the actual, hard PROOF. In some cases, sleep, vitamins, exercise and a good diet will cure so-called "stress or depression." Those mental "disorders" were put down in a book called the "*Diagnostic and Statistical Manual*" for psychiatrists to make a bunch of money by pushing anti-depressants on people. There are no scientific tests that back up these mental diseases that they cite as the causes of your ills. Don't believe me? Go to the Citizens Commission on Human Rights website at: www.cchr.org and find out for yourself.

Think I'm over-reacting? Let's go back to the TV ads. Count the number of ads that show you that you have a "problem" and that the "solution" is that "little green pill." (Uh...Ritalin?) Notice that they end the ad with the phrase, "Ask your doctor about____(insert drug name here)." I saw one TV ad recently that showed a little boy after taking the drug and how obedient he had become--almost like a little robot. Is that the type of child you want to raise? No, me neither. My motto is to let kids be kids and let them run and play and have fun. And I want the same for you—to run and play and have fun and *BE* only who you agree to be!

What does any of this have to do with the American Dream and finances, you ask? What we know so far is that the American Dream is to *BE, DO* and *HAVE* what we want to *BE, DO* and *HAVE*. Most Americans want it. They also want to have control of their finances and their money, and have control of their lives. So by looking at what we have agreed to *BE* because of the influences of the media and the people in our lives, it makes us realize that the things that we have agreed to *BE* may not be decisions we made on our own. We haven't really created our <u>own</u> American Dream at all. We've been trying to live somebody else's.

The GOOD news is that you <u>can</u> change your life by first deciding that YOU and ONLY YOU—not your parents, your spouse, your boss, the doctors, or some TV ad—will decide who and what you are and what you want. The worst thing you can do is lie to yourself and say everything is all right when it isn't. Take a good look at your life and be honest with yourself and recognize how others have influenced your decision-making. It's the only way you can change something that you don't like. Now, if you don't know exactly <u>who</u> you want to *BE* or <u>what</u> you want to achieve, then keep reading, because there are tools that will help you to regain control of your life. How? By helping you find out who you want to *BE*, so you can design the plan to *DO* it, in order to *HAVE* your American Dream.

CHAPTER 6

"Buying" into the Lie

Let's go a little further into the lie. If you've been told that you have to *BE* someone else because you're not good enough as you are, and you have to buy a bunch of stuff to make you that person, then is that the American Dream that you've been searching for? Up to this point, for most of you, it has been.

So how do you do that if you don't have the money?

> Congratulations! You've been pre-approved!
> No annual fee!

That's right. We're now going to talk about how you got that lovely little stack of plastic cards in your wallet. The story begins way back when. Yes, I'll get to the smoking Santa in a little bit. But first, American history, the way you probably <u>didn't</u> learn it in high school.

From Having Nothing to Having Everything

The concept of stuff making you happy can be traced back almost a hundred years. There was a time when Americans pretty much had nothing, and interestingly enough, that time was called a "depression," the Great Depression to be exact. The severe worldwide economic depression that affected all Americans started around 1929 and lasted until the late '30s or early '40s. It's said that the start of the Great Depression was due, in part, to the devastating collapse of U.S. stock market prices on October 29, 1929, known as Black Tuesday. It was the longest, most extensive, and deepest depression of the 20th century. It spread from the U.S. to almost every country in the world. Did you know that? I thought not. You already learned something, carry on.

Unemployment in the U.S. quickly soared to 25 percent, and in some countries rose as high as 33 percent. Countries all around the world were hit hard, especially those dependent on heavy industry such as the United States. Construction was virtually halted in many countries. Farming suffered as crop prices fell.

The Great Depression brought bread lines, soup kitchens, food rations, and thousands of hungry families. Still, people did what they could to make their lives happy. Movies with sound were still new, board games were popular and people gathered around radios to listen to baseball games and short stories. Young people danced to the big band sounds of Sammy Kaye and Guy Lombardo.

Shortages continued throughout World War II, but as men went off to war, women went to work in the factories to help supply aircraft, ships, food, and medicine. The war fueled technological advances, and new jobs were created to meet the demand. When World War II finally ended in 1945, soldiers returned home and the United States began focusing on producing merchandise and agriculture, instead of war material. There was a big jump in the American family income, in quality of life, and improvements in what people were able to obtain in general.

According to www.history.com, almost exactly nine months after World War II ended, "the cry of the baby was heard across the land," as historian Landon Jones later described. More babies were born in 1946 than ever before: 3.4 million, 20 percent more than in 1945. This was the beginning of the so-called "Baby Boom."

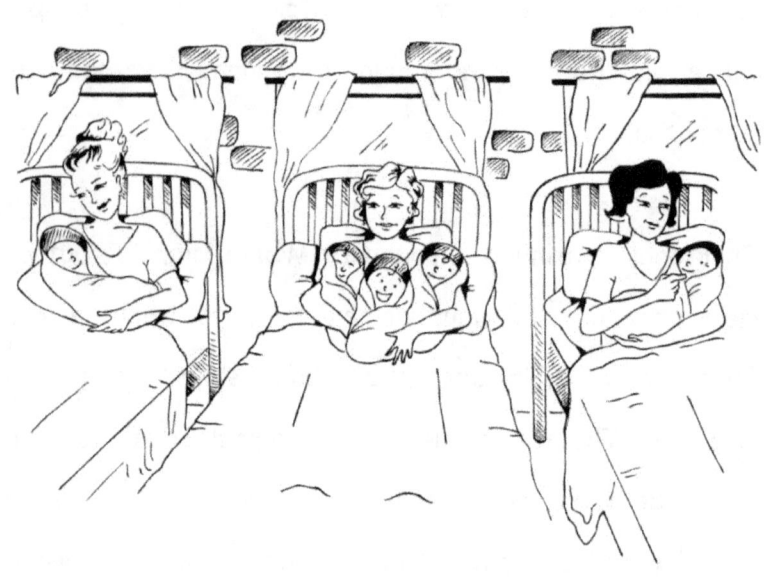

Steve Gillon, who wrote *Boomer Nation,* stated:

"Baby Boom may have been obvious to everyone by 1958, but it caught most Americans by surprise when it started at the end of World War II. In 1946 the census's experts viewed the upsurge in births as temporary and predicted an increase of only 5 million

for the rest of the decade. How wrong they were! In 1948 the nation's mothers gave birth to 4 million babies—a child was born every 8 seconds. By the end of the decade nearly 9 million babies had been born. The census planners had miscalculated by over 50 percent."

He goes on to describe how in 1958 *Life Magazine* called children the "Built-in Recession Cure," concluding that all babies were potential *consumers* who spearheaded "a brand new market for food, clothing and shelter."

By now you may see where I'm headed with this. This generation had a deep effect on our economy and overall, on the "American Dream."

By 1958 America felt it had recovered from the war, the dust had settled, and jobs were in abundance. Families had hope again and it seemed that there was a new invention at every turn. America was thriving. Rock and Roll music was beginning to shape the youth, and television was becoming a standard in most households. The decade of the 1950s is known as "the Golden Age of

Television." *I Love Lucy* debuted along with other entertainment-type programs. Cooking shows and cartoons filled the living rooms of most families. People were purchasing TVs at record speed and by the mid-50s, color television was introduced and everybody had to have one. From the beginning of the 1950s to 1960 consumers had purchased almost 60 million televisions. American business began to take notice of this growing movement and soon discovered the true power of advertising and media.

But before we take a look at that little box known as television (and the story of the smoking Santa), let's get back to this little nugget of American Dream history: how three dudes at dinner set up the system for you to charge all that fun stuff you see advertised on television.

The Creation of the Credit Card

Your gazillion dollar credit card debt all started over cigars and whiskey at a restaurant in New York City, back in 1949.

Three businessmen were having a dinner meeting at Major's Cabin Grill. At the table were Frank X. McNamara, head of Hamilton Credit Corporation, Ralph Schneider, his attorney, and Alfred Bloomingdale (you guessed it, part of the Bloomingdale's empire).

The story goes that the businessmen were discussing a customer-related issue. One of their customers had loaned several of his charge cards to his neighbors and friends in order to help them with their financial difficulties. Gas station and retail stores were issuing cards at this time that had to be paid off every month. When the friends and neighbors couldn't repay him, he was forced to take a loan from the Hamilton Credit Corporation in order to pay back these charge cards.

They finished their meal and when the check arrived for dinner, McNamara reached into his pocket for his wallet only to realize he had left it in his other suit, so he had to call his wife to bring the cash to pay the bill. Between his customer's story and his own experience at the restaurant, a light bulb went on. From there the concept grew, and by 1950 McNamara and his associates had created the Diners' Club card, which is still in existence today. The Diners' Club card was accepted in many other locations and more and more companies were jumping on board to accept it. Their sales increased substantially with the use of that cardboard card. Yes, it was made out of cardboard, not plastic, back in those days.

Now we've all heard the saying, "Nothing in life is free," and the same goes with the Diners' Club card. Any retailer who accepted the card was charged 7 percent for each transaction and the consumers were charged a 3 dollar annual fee. By the end of 1950 more than 20 thousand people were using the Diners' Club card. It wasn't until 1958 that it received competition from Bank of America's BankAmericard and from a company called American Express. *Don't leave home without it.* Apparently nobody did!

Since the creation of the Diners' Club card in 1950, Visa, MasterCard, Discover, and many other companies have entered the scene. According to www.creditcards.com

the number of credit cards in circulation in the U.S. at the end of 2011 was as follows:

- American Express credit: 50.6 million (Source: AmericanExpress.com)
- MasterCard credit: 176 million (Source: MasterCard)
- MasterCard debit: 129 million (Source: MasterCard)
- Visa credit: 261 million, as of Sept. 30, 2011 (Source: Visa)
- Visa debit: 392 million, as of Sept. 30, 2011 (Source: Visa)

If you want to see how fast we're charging up our credit cards, check out the website www.usdebtclock.org. As of April 2, 2012, the national credit card debt was 792 billion dollars. Credit cards have been around for just over 60 years, so how could we have charged that much money? I say it's because advertisers told us that we had to have all of that stuff! What do you think?

Credit card debt is BIG business. As long as you're not paying off your credit cards every month, you're accruing interest charges, and credit card companies are raking in the dough. Interest charges, late fees, annual fees, over-limit fees. Ka-ching ka-ching.

20th Century Advertising

Does advertising have anything to do with the national debt? HELLO?!! It has <u>everything</u> to do with it.

> Okay, NOW we're going to talk about the smoking Santa. Sit up straight and pay attention.

Americans were exposed to the first commercial advertisement on television in the United States back on July 1, 1941. It was a 10-second spot by the Bulova Watch Company that aired on the New York City affiliate WNBT before a baseball game between the Brooklyn Dodgers and the Philadelphia Phillies. According to the website www.thehistoricalarchive.com the commercial was very simple and not much more than a print ad on film that showed a Bulova watch displayed on top of a map of the United States with a voiceover that said, "America runs on Bulova time!" The cost for that commercial was 9 dollars, equivalent in today's economy to about 120 dollars. Many of the commercials to follow included slogans or jingles designed to burn into the average American's everyday thought. Many of these slogans were so successful they're still used today. You've heard them!

"Trust the Midas touch"
from Midas Mufflers

"They're G-r-r-r-eat!"
from Tony the Tiger & Frosted Flakes

"Where's the Beef?"
from Wendy's

"M&M's melt in your mouth, not in your hand,"
from M&Ms

Here's one of my favorites: **"My bologna has a first name it's O-S-C-A-R, my bologna has a second name it's M-A-Y-E-R! Oh I love to eat it every day and if you ask me why I'll say, 'cause Oscar Mayer has a way with b-o-l-o-g-n-a."**

In 1973 Oscar Mayer came out with a commercial of the cutest little boy, sitting on a dock, fishing, eating a bologna sandwich, and singing this jingle. I LOVED that commercial and to this day can recite it perfectly. That's what you call advertising that <u>sticks</u> with you.

Most of the advertising in the 1950s was focused towards women, because after World War II men returned home and women left their factory jobs to resume their positions in the household. At that time "a woman's place was in the home," some said. They raised families, they cooked and they cleaned. The TV show *I Love Lucy* portrayed that world, and to this day I watch *I Love Lucy* reruns because life seemed to be so much simpler back then. But also because she is hysterical and makes me laugh.

Television was still new in the '50s and most products being advertised were being purchased by American consumers at a rapid rate.

Advertisers began to realize that due to the many similar types of products out there, commercials were most effective in helping the consumer swing in favor of one particular brand. Think about it. Do you know what the difference is between Fab Detergent and Bold Detergent? What if the "Fab" brand commercial told you that Fab could "Make your clothes smell better!" Would you buy that brand? I know I like to smell good!

I know you understand this concept because you've seen all the different types of products out there. Have you walked down the cereal aisle in the grocery store lately? There are dozens of cereals, even though most are made by one of three companies: General Mills, Post or Kellogg. Don't get me wrong—I like variety. But come on, how many different brands of "new and improved" bran cereal with raisins do you need? With so many choices, sometimes we can't make a decision, so we end up buying several different kinds and have an out-of-control grocery bill. I know I've done it! The products are endless and Americans have to choose which one is right for them, and the most successful advertisers with the deepest pockets make it easier for us to make those decisions in their favor.

Advertising at that time was in its prime. The shift from newspaper, magazine and radio to television ads began to echo powerfully with consumers. These advertising agencies were literally fighting to create ads that "helped" consumers figure out what they "needed" in order to live a certain lifestyle. They built research facilities, observational study groups and test groups; they hired writers, and filled rooms with artists and actors to help create a new wave of commercials.

Advertisers were literally selling a slice of the "American Dream" even if it was just a dishwasher, a car, fancy makeup, or a pack of cigarettes.

Yes, I'm going to talk about the smoking Santa soon.

These ads set the standard for "the good life." The consumer's awareness was saturated with campaigns that were designed to be repetitive, catchy, attractive, and convincing to Americans to persuade them to purchase a certain product.

A perfect example of deceptive advertising during the 1950s would have to be cigarettes. According to www.smokingstatistics.org: *"1950 was a significant year for cigarette manufacturers and cigarette consumers, for it was during that year that a major study showed the link between smoking and lung cancer. Understandably, this was an important medical finding, and it was published at a time when it was estimated that more than half of the United States' population smoked."*

Can you imagine if half of all Americans smoked these days? From the research I've done, less than 20 percent of Americans currently smoke cigarettes. I live in California, one of the states with many anti-smoking laws, including no smoking in public buildings, workplaces, in or near restaurants, and in some places, no smoking outside—period!

If people still had the old habits of 1950, there'd be so much second-hand smoke that someone would have to develop a device that went over your head or that you blew through to make it so there was no smoke anywhere. Could you imagine such a contraption? Well, I sure could:

Even with that 1950 medical finding linking cigarettes and lung cancer, the tobacco industry continued to deny the allegations and promoted their brands with dedication. After all, smoking cigarettes was publicized as the "cool thing to do." It was socially acceptable and the majority of men and women smoked. It was even acceptable for pregnant women to smoke. In most cases you'd probably be smoking while waiting in the doctor's office for your check-up; your doctor might even light your cigarette for you. Television started an explosion of ads from tobacco companies. Madison Avenue hired the best of the best to get their ads out there. Consumers were deceived, and how! Ads containing doctors, beautiful women, cowboys, babies, cartoon characters, and yes, **even Santa Claus** was used to get consumers to buy. It wasn't until 1969 that tobacco advertising was banned from broadcast media. Here's an example of an incredible ad that was actually used back in the day of Santa smoking a Pall Mall:

So much has changed since the 1950s. Women now know that it's not healthy to smoke while pregnant and even cowboys get lung cancer. It's proven that Coca-Cola isn't healthy for an infant to drink, and women can do more than just cook, clean and raise the kids. But in that same sense we now have more avenues of advertising than ever before. With the dawn of the internet, satellite radio, iPads, YouTube and minicomputer-like cell phones, the advertiser's reach to consumers pushing some "American Dream" product is endless, and in essence, less censored. And that's where the marriage of American Dream myths and endless credit card spending takes place.

Back in the 1950s, when most Americans bought something, they paid in full for it, right then and there. Some used store credit cards, but those still had to be paid fully within 30 days. People thought borrowing money was a risky move that could lead to financial ruin. During that era one income per household was enough for the family to live on, compared to today where it generally takes two incomes to pay for the normal family lifestyle. There wasn't the need to borrow due to economic fluctuation; the '50s were a time that enjoyed the highest standard of living in the world.

Robert Sarnoff, founder of the NBC, said in 1956, *"The reason we have such a high standard of living, is because advertising has created an American frame of mind that makes people want more things, better things, and newer things."* Isn't that the truth?

The '60s

The 1960s could best be described as the decade for social revolution and freedom. John F. Kennedy was elected president, the first man walked on the moon, Martin Luther King, Jr. fought for civil rights, feminists fought for equal rights for women, and how can we forget Woodstock! Unfortunately this decade had its fair share of struggles too, with Vietnam and the assassinations of President Kennedy and Martin Luther King, Jr. to name three of the biggest.

Despite the turmoil of this new era, the early 1960s were a time of recovery and economic growth. American families were able to live the comfortable life that was portrayed on posters, magazines, movies and television shows. More families were able to afford cars, which also meant that families could move to the suburbs, and new housing developments took off.

With jobs in abundance, the father of the household could afford the material possessions that his wife, son or daughter wanted, rather than needed. Finally they were able to achieve the idealism of the "perfect family" also known as the "Nuclear Family"—Mom, Dad and two kids—the images which advertisers and marketers supplied in newspapers and magazines, on radio and television.

What we consider today to be necessary appliances in any household—such as a refrigerator, vacuum cleaner, and a washer/dryer—haven't always been so easily attainable! By the '60s, most households did have black and white television sets, which they gladly watched as a family activity in the evenings.

In the '60s, it became more and more acceptable for women to work. Even a wife and mother could get a job working one or two mornings a week doing typical secretarial or typing duties. This provided a small source of income for her to buy certain things for herself or her family.

During the summer months, school was out and family vacations were becoming more popular. Gasoline was still relatively cheap and new highway systems were being built all across the nation in one of the largest public spending projects in the country's history. Hotels and motels were popping up and becoming popular to this new trend of vacationers.

It seemed every family was competing to be the envy of their neighborhood. They compared themselves to others who had the consistently manicured yard, newest car, best recipes, most social activities, better educated child or prettier wife, which also gave rise to body enhancements and spa visits. Consumers were filling up on a slice of the old American pie, often referred to as the "American Dream." And it was advertising that spearheaded this new campaign for consumerism.

However, all these expenses came with a price. And I don't mean just long hours and weekends at the job for Mr. Smith. Typically the most common payment method during the early 20th century was cash or personal check. There was no "buy on credit" and make minimum payments for 20 years. By the late 1960's banking companies thought of the brilliant idea of mailing out unsolicited credit cards to millions of Americans, and the rest is history.

Shark Attack!

Aside from credit cards, department store and gas cards, and bank loans, consumers could also borrow money, if needed, from loan sharks. We're all familiar with the concept you've seen in Hollywood movies. The loan shark usually worked for the mob and would loan you money with your body as collateral. The story goes that if you didn't pay him back he'd begin with threats and ultimately end up breaking a leg or a few fingers in order to get paid. But was that _really_ the case?

Loan sharks actually operated on a slight business level. They had offices and in most cases they didn't lend money to just an average gambler or criminal. They loaned money to the everyday husband, businessman or consumer who had a steady income or respectable job. They typically had the consumer sign a contract, and although the contract wasn't actually a legally binding document, it was still evidence of the loan, which the lender could use as blackmail in order to expedite payment.

Having these sorts of lending operations, although illegal, were quite common. In most cases if a debtor didn't pay back the loan quickly, the loan shark would begin to threaten them with legal action. They knew that most people who borrowed the money couldn't afford an attorney to defend them in court, so the threats were successful. Additionally if someone didn't pay back the loan, they resorted to other methods of intimidation, such as going to their home, paying a visit to their neighbors and ringing their phones off the hook, harassing their wives or other family members.

If that didn't work, they would threaten to complain to the borrower's employer. Now keep in mind, back in those days most companies forbid their employees from getting these types of loans and if their employer found out, they would fire them.

Most people who borrowed from loan sharks were folks who had been turned down by licensed lenders due to low income or various other reasons. Loan sharks got paid handsomely because of ridiculously high interest rates and late fees that they were able to charge.

But most consumers avoided the loan sharks and chose the simpler, less-threatening form of debt — the credit card.

By 1969 the magnetic strip was developed, and within a couple of years, it was on every credit card being printed. Despite several recessions in 1957, 1960 and 1969, Americans were able to purchase more products faster by using credit cards.

The '70s

The 1970s recession was a direct reflection and result of the activism from the '60s. Vietnam ended in 1973 but still reverberated years later. Veterans were shocked by the cold and unsympathetic reception they received when they returned home. There were protests and riots at airports and train stations. Veterans were considered to be outsiders, psychologically damaged, dangerous citizens. It wasn't until the late '70s that society began to treat the Vietnam veteran as victims of the war instead of being the perpetrators of it.

As veterans returned home they encountered a loss of jobs. Our country hadn't been prepared for the returning soldiers. Baby Boomer children were entering the work force and unemployment was at an all-time high. Even by today's standards, the '70s could be considered the worst decade of unemployment.

Let's not forget the gas crisis during the early and late '70s. The cost of gasoline went from an average 38 cents to 55 cents within a year. Gas stations were being asked not to sell gas on Saturday nights or Sundays and most stations complied. People were only able to get gas on their day of the week. If the last number of your license was an odd number, then you were only able to get gas on Monday, Wednesday and Friday and if your number was even then you were able to get gas on the other three days that week. This resulted in long lines and people re-evaluated weekend getaways or trips. I remember sitting in lines for hours on my day to get gas. People would run out of gas sitting in line and have to push their cars down the street and into the station to fill up. Some would be late to work and lose their jobs because of the gas crisis. By the end of the '70s gas was nearly one dollar a gallon. Sounds ridiculously low now, but back then one dollar was a lot of money.

As a result of our dependency on foreign oil, also known as "black gold," we soon found that we were running low on other types of energy, fueled by gas and oil. Throughout the early '70s the government took several steps to conserve energy. By 1973 there were moves made to ban Christmas lights, enforce thermostat temperatures and hours of operation in offices and schools, and conduct random power outages to preserve energy. So here's my question: If we had such shortages then—and it's now more than 40 years and millions of people later—was there _really_ a shortage back then? Or was it the government putting limitations and controls on us? Just a question that I've had for years.

The Arrival of the Bill Collector

With credit card debt on the rise, there grew a new demand for debt collection. But keep in mind, as long as there has been money, there have been debtors, and someone chasing them to pay up.

In 1977 Congress passed a bill known as the Fair Debt Collection Practices Act (FDCPA). The act limits how and when a collector can contact debtors to recover an amount owed. Prior to this bill, the debt collection industry was like the Wild West. Most of the debt collectors from that era would use any collection method or technique they could think of, even if it was illegal, immoral or downright deceiving. And because most of these companies were small businesses, the states lacked the laws that would protect consumers from this type of behavior.

I remember years ago when I worked at a collection agency, I got quite an education. The manager at the time had been a bill collector prior to the FDCPA. The things he told me that they used to do would make your skin crawl. He said they would threaten a debtor's family with physical harm if they didn't pay the bill. Sometimes they would go to people's houses and literally beat them up, or go with shotguns drawn and make them pay. I remember one story he told me where he had the debtor so upset that he literally offered him one of his children if he would go away. The collection manager was so shocked that he backed down and didn't go visit that man again. Can you imagine that? I couldn't!

It wasn't until the 1980s that the debt collection industry really took off. At that time the government needed a source of collection for all of the bad student loans. We're talking millions of dollars in student loans! The small collection agencies couldn't supply the services that the government needed. As a result, larger collection firms began to emerge. Before you knew it, companies were contracting companies from overseas to do our dirty work. There was a LOT of debt to collect.

The '80s

The '80s could be considered the decade for excess and self-indulgence, which, if you compared it to the '60s, was quite the opposite. During the '60s Americans were politically active, marching, exercising their freedom of speech, and fighting for the rights of <u>all</u>, including equality for women and minorities. Back then it was your duty to vote, your duty to stand up for what was right, and Americans, especially the youth, did so in droves. You've heard the saying, "Power to the people!" For many during the '80s, the slogan might have been something more like "Power to the person!" It was no longer about society as a whole or a group, but rather for the individuals themselves.

By 1980 Americans were tired. No longer was it about working together for common goals or achievements, it was about "me." Those Baby Boomers who were born after World War II were between the ages of 20 and 34. They weren't adults who feared a Great Depression, were rationed food, or had bomb shelters under their houses. They weren't forced to group together for the greater good. They weren't really aware of the difficulties their parents had endured, unless they heard the stories from Uncle Pete or Grandpa Joe. And how many of those old stories did they want to hear anyway? I know that for me, when someone would start telling a story during a holiday, I was the first to leave the room.

It was an era of technological advances. By then most American households had more sophisticated televisions. Cable TV, individual TV programs and entire channels catering to <u>each</u> family member hit America's living rooms: MTV for teens, cartoons for the children, *the A-Team* or *MacGyver* for Dad and perhaps *The Love Boat* and *Fantasy Island* for Mom. More TV channels, programs, and commercials for everyone! And it gets better. With the invention of remote control, there was no longer a need to get up and turn the knob to change channels.

Technology really boomed. Soon there were cassettes instead of 8-track tapes, VCRs so we could record our favorite programs or movies, the first cellular mobile phone arrived (so big that it could double as a paperweight), video games popped up and let's not forget PERSONAL COMPUTERS! Computers were finally geared toward the not so technically-savvy users.

It was no longer just an item for the office; families were purchasing computers for the home. In the beginning the computers were pretty basic, and so were video games. However, by the end of the decade both products had developed into higher quality, with more complicated systems and better overall performance. The business world was changing rapidly as well, with mergers, bank buyouts and corporate takeovers. A new kind of millionaire popped up. Bill Gates and Donald Trump soon became popular household names, and people tuned into the TV show, *Lifestyles of the Rich and Famous*.

I still remember the catchy signature phrase, "Champagne wishes and caviar dreams!" Americans sure were dreaming. And <u>everyone</u> wanted a slice of the pie.

While executive salaries skyrocketed during the '80s, allowing people to enjoy the world of champagne and caviar, the average American working in industries such as coal, shipbuilding, steel, and car manufacturing, experienced quite the opposite. Presidents Reagan and Bush froze the minimum wage for <u>nine years</u>, essentially giving the average worker a pay <u>cut</u> each year as inflation ate into their paychecks.

How could Americans afford all of those extravagant new luxuries that advertisers were promoting so heavily on TV shows and elsewhere? *That little plastic thing in their wallet,* that's how.

By 1980 it was estimated that almost 18 percent of Americans had at least one credit card. The new plastic cards with that cool magnetic strip on the back, made purchases faster and easier than before. Swipe 'n go. And boy, did we! In the beginning, banks and other card issuers offered low interest rates to get people to run up their debt on those little cards. But the days of low interest rates would be short-lived. And here's <u>why</u>.

Interest Rates, Unlimited

In the late '70s and early '80s Citibank, one of the largest credit card companies at the time, was going bankrupt because New York had strict laws on how much interest they could charge consumers. Citibank realized they were losing money on credit cards. It was costing more to provide the credit than they could earn back from consumers.

Have you ever wondered why your credit card statement comes from South Dakota even though you know your bank is located elsewhere, in particular New York? By some bizarre stroke of fate, the economy of South

Dakota was also hitting hard times. At the time South Dakota didn't have an interest rate cap at all. A person could be charged any interest rate whatsoever. Citibank found this out. They contacted the governor and the resulting deal allowed Citibank to move their credit card operations to South Dakota. This move eventually brought South Dakota more than 3,000 high-paying jobs, which helped save South Dakota's failing economy.

Soon Citibank was able to charge their customers any amount of interest they wanted, which is exactly what they did. Between 1980 and 1990, the number of credit cards nearly doubled, and consumers were willing to pay any interest rate they were charged so that they could buy what they wanted. Other banks followed suit and moved to South Dakota or to the state of Delaware which also changed its laws to uncap interest rates.

How is this possible, you ask? Due to a combination of federal laws and 50 different state laws, a bank in New York is allowed to use a South Dakota address to bill a customer in California. Shady? Slimy? Well, it doesn't matter what I think because by law they can do it.

So there you have it: South Dakota was the beginning of it all. Massive interest charges, dangerous annual fees, and all sorts of other charges they could squeeze out of the consumer. How's that for your constitutional rights? And in case you were wondering about the laws in <u>your</u> state, check out: <u>www.usurylaw.com</u>.

The '90s

When the '90s came around we'd already gone through our technological advances and it <u>seemed</u> all was well. Most people had credit cards and were buying homes, fancy cars, vacations and other such luxuries. Let's all play like we're rich! However, unlike many of our grandparents, who only bought what they could pay for in cash or knew they could AFFORD over a long-term period, the '90s were about <u>quick cash</u>: how to get it and how to spend it.   And the new technology made it so *easy.*

In the '90s it seemed computers and the internet were driving America forward. Although the "official" internet had been around for awhile, it wasn't until the early to mid '90s that it finally became available to everyday people. And, as with most inventions, people began to think about the advantages of this new form of faster, easier, FREE communication. Ask anyone over 30 and they'll describe that annoying dial-up sound: beeeep...phsshhhh...brwaarrrr...pppshhhh. Wait five minutes and yep, the internet! It used to drive me nuts waiting for the old dial-up system to connect. Then if someone called, the internet connection would be cut and I would have to start all over again. I'm glad someone solved that!

Advertisers, small businesses, investors, and multi-millionaires all scrambled to take advantage of the new, free web pages, chat rooms, and message boards. New college graduates and nerds alike became instant millionaires with their "dot-com" businesses. All types of companies popped up online, promising food delivery, pet supplies, and things like "internet cash," which was sort of like *Monopoly* money, but to be used on the internet. Many of these companies actually ended up filing bankruptcy or failing altogether by the year 2000, when the "dot-com bubble" burst.

Fast Cash Online

Initially people believed that the internet should be non-commercial. However by the mid '90s that idea changed and websites began advertising products and services, including (sound the horns) payday loans and cash advances! You've probably heard the ads on TV or radio promising "quick cash" with no credit check required. "Get Instantly Approved!" was the pitch for a cash advance loan against your paycheck.

Although obtaining a payday loan is quite easy, paying it back with all the extra fees attached is another story. While each state has its own laws on how much interest the loan companies can charge you (for details check www.paydayloaninfo.org), in most cases the average loan term is about two weeks and the interest rate can be as high as 38 to 57 percent. Yes, you read that right—it's not a typo. Some states have made it illegal to offer payday loans because of the exorbitant fees that they can charge. Typically the amounts borrowed range from $100 to $1000, and sometimes more.

Here's an example of how this works: Your electricity is going to be shut off tomorrow due to non-payment, but you don't get paid for another four days. What do you do? Your credit is horrible and you would be humiliated asking a friend or family member for money. So you decide to take out a loan for $100 from a payday loan company. Now here's the tricky and sometimes dangerous part. In most cases you have to provide a copy of your paycheck in order to get approved for the loan and you have to give them a blank check from your checking account. They fill it in later and deposit it on your next payday, so you can pay them back. However, let's say that you took out the payday loan with the _hopes_ that you could pay it back the following week, but when that time comes you don't have the money in your account, so the check you sent in bounces. Remember, YOU gave them the authorization to send it through, which means if it bounces, YOU'RE the one on the hook for it. Yes, writing a bad check will accumulate more fees from your bank for the returned item. Now even though you may not have intended it to bounce, some lenders will threaten you with criminal action for failing to make good on a check. They may also take it upon themselves to sue for damages under civil bad check laws. And no one likes to get sued.

So now you're unable to pay back the loan when you said you would. What to do? You decide to pay the "renewal fee" of $20 to buy another week, but you still owe the original $100. In addition, they charged you a penalty fee of, let's say $35, which they added to your bill. Whoa! You now owe $135 and paid 20 bucks to extend the loan. Here's the worst part: If you continued doing this for several weeks, you could end up paying roughly

$200 or more. This means you paid more than double the original amount owed. The horror stories of how many consumers have been caught in this trap and end up spending thousands of dollars are abundant.

Although payday loans were not as widespread back in the early '90s as they are today, the industry has been growing at a record rate. In an article called "The Growth of Legal Loan Sharking" published in November 1998 by Jean Ann Fox of the Consumer Federation of America, she explains this growing trend, and what kind of consumers these companies prey upon: *"The market for payday loans is made up of consumers who have personal checking accounts, but who are stretched to the limit financially. These consumers are not even living paycheck to paycheck, but are borrowing against their next paycheck to meet living expenses. Ace Cash Express' Vice President says payday loan customers "tend to be people at the bottom of the middle-class structure in this country."*

Well I don't know about you, but I don't want to be considered someone who is at the bottom of the barrel for not being able to make ends meet. Because here's the irony of it: If these people are so bad off, then why does the industry charge them more fees than any other credit limit or card? It just makes it <u>worse</u> for them, doesn't it? Of course because they're a high credit risk, companies can charge them more interest, particularly since the consumer probably can't get any other type of loan. But wouldn't it make more sense to help consumers by advancing money <u>cheaply</u> so that they can actually make ends meet and stop getting the loans? Yes it would, but who is going to convince the payday loan companies of this? And how many of them are going to listen? That's right, NONE!

Applying online for such a loan is dangerous as it leaves you open to security and fraud issues. So, with that being said, let's all agree to stay away from payday loans. Agreed? Say yes! Thank you!

Ads Everywhere

As inflation grew in the '90s, so did advertisements promoting all the new things that we "needed" to buy. Television commercials, radio ads, magazines, posters, billboards, and the new internet crammed our everyday lives with images and messages of how these things would improve this or improve that, or help you be this or be that.

The average family saw its credit card debt <u>double</u> in the '90s alone. And bankruptcies, both personal and professional, soon followed. The idea of paying for something with cash seemed to be a foreign concept in the '90s, and I'm sure our grandparents would have scolded us for spending this way, if they only knew what we were doing.

With so many credit card companies competing for your business, they knew how to make their product stand out. You could qualify to get a card at the level of Platinum, Gold or other "statuses." Your credit card was supposed to be a direct representation of your financial wealth.

In 1999, American Express introduced (again, sound the horns!) the <u>Centurion Card</u>, referred to as the "black card." This card was meant for the more affluent, financially well-off individual. It had no cap on how much you could charge, and you didn't apply for it—it was and still is by invitation only. American Express promoted the card as "Rarely seen, always recognized."

Now let's be real—the Centurion Card was not for middle-class Americans. But average American citizens still had plenty of credit card companies competing for their business. The plan was for you to buy things you couldn't afford so that they could charge you more interest. Then your bill would be so large that you could only make the minimum monthly payments, hence you'd continue to be a customer with them for <u>years,</u> as you slowly pay off that debt.

American household spending has served as the main force of U.S. economic growth for some time. The efforts made to get consumers to buy were heavily dependent on this idea. After all, we were told in the '50s and '60s to help our country by stimulating the economy by buying stuff, and we did so with fervor. In fact, if we didn't have the money, we just borrowed more money! Heck put it on credit! However this spending spree has since snowballed out of control. Companies, industries and entire <u>countries</u> have become dependent on our spending.

2000: The Hole Gets Deeper

The new millennium saw its fair share of advertising. The number of products that were produced having to do with the so-called "Y2K" disaster was ridiculous. Remember when we were told that all computers on earth were going to break because their clocks wouldn't change over correctly at the beginning of the year 2000? And how none of them actually failed? The Y2K frenzy had everybody scared and running out to buy new computers that wouldn't break. Consumers spent a fortune on turn of the century items because there was so much hype about it. According to the Federal

Reserve (www.federalreserve.com), by the year 2000 the total credit card debt for America was a staggering 702 billion dollars compared to 39 billion dollars in 1977. Debt collection was big business as the larger debt collection companies bought up smaller companies. This frenzy of mergers evolved into something like *The Blob* (1958 horror movie), producing massive and sometimes untouchable juggernauts in the debt collection industry.

Many of us unfortunately have had to deal with a debt collector at one point or another. How it works is simple. Say you owe money to American Express. After being delinquent so many months, they send your account to a collection agency which attempts to collect from you until an arrangement is worked out and payment is received. The collection agency gets a cut of the amount paid and the rest goes to American Express. In some cases, American Express may sell your account to another agency which will get 100 percent of the recouped money. You have to realize that when they sell your account, it's usually for a few cents on the dollar. So even with a minimal settlement from you, the company will make money.

If you've ever dealt with a debt collector or heard stories, you know it can be an uncomfortable and sometimes humiliating experience. Some of the collectors curse, some threaten to sue, and some claim they work for law enforcement, saying they'll arrest you unless you pay up immediately. They'll do <u>anything</u> to get their commission. But let's get one thing straight: Debts are a <u>civil</u> matter, not a <u>criminal</u> matter. You can't go to jail for owing money to a credit card company. It's important you know this. KNOW YOUR CONSUMER RIGHTS ABOUT DEBT COLLECTION.

Check out the <u>Fair Debt Collection Practices Act</u> (FDCPA) which you can view at <u>www.ftc.gov</u>.

Mistaking Your Home for a Wallet

Now let's address the American Dream myth that totally blew up in the new millennium—owning your own home and then using it to borrow even more money to buy even more things.

With housing prices at their highest in history many families were refinancing their homes or taking out lines of credit for home improvements or personal consumption. This was known as the "Housing Bubble." Many did so in hopes of adding even more value to their homes by replacing entire kitchens or making other improvements. Or perhaps they used their home equity loans to pay off the credit card debt they incurred while fixing their homes. I've talked to a lot of these people who did pay off their credit cards, and then charged them right back up again. People also used the money from their homes to buy boats, vacations, new cars, or whatever they wanted. Some pulled money from the equity in their homes to buy second or third homes. It got pretty out of control.

In addition to families buying existing homes in excess, new development was at an all-time high. It seemed that everywhere you turned, new houses and businesses were being built. The housing market was on steroids and America was on a high, with no sobriety in sight. Times were good. Americans were living the dream. "Houses for everyone!" Well at least for most.

While many have their theories on what caused the Housing Bubble, most will agree that one of the underlying causes had to do with the big banks. Banks were handing out mortgage loans to many customers who simply weren't credit-worthy, approving loans to buyers who they knew wouldn't be able to afford the loan in the long run. And to make matters worse, the banks were handing out loans with no down payments, or without running proper background checks such as proof of employment or income. Many of the buyers were told they could buy the house and make interest-only payments for three years and perhaps refinance later when things got better. However, at the end of the three year period, most home owners hadn't seen much change to their income and when it came time to pay the actual mortgage payment (not interest-only payments) they couldn't afford them. For instance, some folks tried refinancing, as their brokers had originally recommended, only to find that the housing market had changed and they couldn't get approved by their banks.

As fate proved obvious, these same un-creditworthy customers soon defaulted on the loans and America saw a new onslaught of foreclosures and bankruptcies. Development on new homes began to slow and in a few years came to an abrupt halt. And as with any slowdown in an industry, so came the loss of jobs.

Any smart homeowner knows that when times get tough, you have to trim the fat. So what bills do you think strapped homeowners stopped paying first, before their mortgage payment? The credit card bills, of course.

Creative Debt Management

Another interesting thing happened in the new millennium: companies popped up everywhere to help people with their debt. First there was the Consumer Credit Counseling Service (CCCS). They helped people by negotiating with banks, utilities, and other creditors to lower their interest rates or balances, consolidating all their outstanding accounts into one easy monthly payment, and counseled consumers on how to better handle their finances. I know that CCCS was around long before the new millennium, but it got very popular during this time because consumers were out of options to handle their debt.

The industry was going strong until the federal government decided to do an investigation on the industry. At the time, most of the companies were stating they were "non-profit" to get more consumers to sign up. The federal government shut down several of those companies or took away their non-profit statuses. Around the same time, banks decided to do their own credit counseling and some of them stopped accepting outside programs altogether. Even though there are still companies out there doing CCCS, it's not as popular or successful as it once was. If you're shopping for help, you can get a list of approved credit counseling agencies at the United States Department of Justice website at: www.justice.gov. However, I wouldn't advise going through a CCCS company because their success rate is minimal. The number of consumers who actually get through a CCCS program is very low.

Next in the new millennium, "Credit Repair" or "Credit Restoration" companies cropped up, promising to fix your credit so that you could buy a house. How? They would send so many letters to the credit bureaus to dispute entries on your credit report that the bureaus would take the bad item off of your credit report—at least for a short time, maybe a month or so. It was enough time for your credit score to go up so you could quickly get approved for a loan to buy a house before the bad credit item was put back on your report. In most cases these credit repair companies couldn't really do what they claimed they could do. Only a legitimately old or wrong item can come off of your credit report.

The federal government created several laws addressing this part of the industry to try to protect consumers. It's easy to get things off of your credit report if you know what to do.   When you go online and get your report, there are instructions on how to get something removed. If it's wrong, then you can get it removed. If it's legitimate, then it will stay there for a certain amount of time.

There was also an industry that sprung up to specifically help people consolidate their student loans.   This industry was very successful in helping consumers consolidate all of their student loans into one payment instead of many. The federal government completely closed down that industry.

Then the debt settlement industry popped up. Companies were helping consumers by settling debts for a percentage of the amount owed. People who were too far in debt and couldn't pay could go into one of these programs for help.   When the mortgage industry crashed; many of the mortgage brokers who were used to making six-figure incomes slid over into the debt settlement industry. They started signing up people by the truckload, but they didn't know how to do debt settlement and that caused a lot of consumer complaints.

At the same time, loan modifications started to get popular because people were losing their homes over those bad mortgages. This new financial tool promised to help them keep a roof over their heads by modifying their home loans so that the monthly mortgage payments were more affordable. Customers were going into debt settlement programs to handle their credit card bills and "loan mod" programs to save their homes.

In October 2010, the federal government passed a law making it almost impossible to do debt settlement. Companies charging upfront fees were now being told that they had to provide the service for free, and only receive payment after the debt was fully settled. Most debt settlement companies, accustomed to other procedures, couldn't adjust to the new laws and went out of business. This left a lot of consumers high and dry and in worse shape than before they started. The federal government also came in and shut down numerous loan modification companies, again leaving consumers to handle their own mortgages. As the recession deepened, many homeowners searched for help and found none; they lost their homes to the banks which were selling them off. There was very little help in sight.

New bankruptcy laws were also passed during the new millennium, making it more difficult to file bankruptcy. Besides filling out a very tall stack of forms to even file for Chapter 7 or Chapter 13 bankruptcy, there is now a clause in the new law which states that you must go through a financial education program to learn to better manage your money before you can file for bankruptcy.

There are also companies that have sprung up that are suing credit card companies to try to get their clients' debts forgiven. It is very difficult to operate in an industry that helps people with their finances today. I've even seen attorneys disbarred recently for helping consumers with their credit card debt or home loans. You can find these online by going to the www.ftc.gov

website for information on companies that have been shut down.

CHAPTER 7

Waking up from the Dream

I could go on and on about how the banks refused to negotiate new loan terms with lower rates so homeowners could keep their homes. I could go on and on about how the banks got a bailout and consumers were left in the dust. I could go on and on about how credit card companies refused to work with folks who had been hit by hard times, or how shady companies that pretended to help consumers with their debt didn't. Or I could go on and on about all of the legitimate companies that were trying to help consumers but got shut down by the federal government anyway. But agreeing that we've all been *victimized* won't get any of us out of the muck. So instead I ask:

> Who charged the debt and/or signed up for that mortgage that they couldn't afford in the first place?

You didn't <u>have</u> to sign on the dotted line, now did you? I know, this is a hard pill to swallow because sometimes it's easier to blame somebody else. But the truth of the matter is—<u>you</u> got all of that stuff that put you in debt and now <u>you</u> have to get yourself out of it. The bank isn't going to come to your rescue on this, and if they do give you a loan to pay everything off, it's not going to be free.

I'm not pointing fingers, because we've <u>all</u> done it. We charged up our credit cards. We spent the money, we bought the toys, we paid for the vacations and/or the remodeling of the house. We did this. Just because banks handed out home loans like *Monopoly* money or credit cards like candy, ultimately it was Americans themselves who spent all that money that they didn't have.

So how do we wake up from this "American Dream" that has turned into a debt nightmare?

> **Start paying attention,**
> **and question what you're told.**

I read a very interesting article in the *Los Angeles Times* the other day about oil changes for cars. It said that your vehicle actually doesn't need an oil change every 3,000 miles. I didn't know this, did you? I'm not particularly mechanically inclined, but I am one of those people who gets my oil changed every 3,000 miles, without fail. The article said that a car only needs an oil change every 7,500-10,000 miles. My eyes popped out of my head. I've been paying $40 every three months when really I only need to change my oil every eight months or so? I was peeved! In fact, those Jiffy Lube commercials kept ringing in my head.

The article went on to explain that the State of California is launching a campaign to stop drivers from consuming so much oil. The State even set up a website where drivers can look up suggested motor oil changes for your type of car: www.checkyournumber.org.

So, what's the point of me telling you this story? Simple. Somehow I was deceived by all of those Jiffy Lube commercials, thinking I "needed" an oil change every 3,000 miles, when in reality I didn't.

I never even questioned what I heard on the commercial. They had the experts, right? Seems small, but this is the point I'm trying to make, dear readers. I too, was scammed by clever, well-thought-out marketing and advertising into thinking I needed something that I really didn't.

Unfortunately, sometimes I think consumers <u>know</u> they're being manipulated, yet choose to continue to purchase anyway. I think this is where most of us get caught up in this debt trap. We buy the fancy car or the most modern home, have the best vacations, become the well-dressed family, have the newest stainless steel 'fridge, get in on the Black Friday deals, *HAVE* the "this" and "that." The list goes on and on. How many of us have ever stopped our undying urge to purchase something and asked ourselves:

> **"Do I actually <u>need</u> all this stuff?"**

I do believe it's okay to buy nice things for yourself and your family. I do believe it's okay to go to the movies and eat out at a fancy restaurant. I also believe that vacations with the family are one of the great joys in life. So don't deprive yourself of those things that you love. That's not what I'm trying to communicate here. Just make sure that any decision you make about spending money is one you make on your own, awake and aware of what you're doing. If you decide to live within your means and you want to take that dream vacation to Paris then save up for it and pay cash.

By doing this, you're <u>setting a goal</u> to <u>achieve a specific dream</u>. You're looking forward to something, you're planning it, you're working towards it, and when you achieve the goal—sipping your latte at the Eiffel

Tower—you'll enjoy it _fully_, without worrying about it afterward, because there will be no huge debt to deal with later. It's PAID IN FULL! Oo la la what a concept.

CHAPTER 8

<u>Whose Stuff is it Anyway?</u>

As you can see from our look back at the history of consumer spending in America, falling for the advertising pitch that we need everything that's big, shiny, and better, without being able to really <u>afford</u> it, has gotten us up to our necks in debt. And that pitch continues 24-7, everywhere we look.

I don't believe that I must have the latest electronic gizmo upgrade the minute it comes out, or the most powerful doodad or the shiniest thingamajig. I'll admit that the enticements are getting harder and harder to resist because they're so pretty or powerful, and they make me look like I have something spectacular. If you're in the financial position to have these things and don't accumulate debt in the process of acquiring them, then by all means, if that's what you want, get them. But make sure that everything else is paid and you can afford the new items. Believe me, it is nice to have nice things; it makes me feel good. But we also have to realize that those nice things come at a price—and paying that price can be difficult and not always worth it in the long run.

Take a 35-inch flat screen TV. You can get one for $200 or $300 nowadays. Not bad, right? Well if you pay the $200 or $300, plus tax in most states, your TV will cost you about $294.92. But if you put it on that Visa card with an interest rate of 19 percent or higher, then only make minimum or small payments, you'll be paying hundreds more for that TV, and you'll be paying on that card for years. You had to buy it because it was (horns and drum roll please) ON SALE!!!

The Ownership Trap

Let's look at this for a minute. If you pay $500 cash for something, then you're out $500 and you own that thing free and clear. If you buy it on credit, technically the bank that issued you the credit card owns it. Now in most states they won't come and repossess the TV or some other such item. Even though it's sitting in your living room, you don't really "own" it, and if you stop making payments on it, then you may really feel like it doesn't belong to you. Let me give you an example:

A friend of mine bought an entertainment center on credit. She got a TV, a DVD player and a game system for her kids. She said that she and the kids loved the system and played with it often. Shortly after she purchased it she lost her job and stopped paying on her credit card. She noticed that right after she missed the due date on her card, the kids stopped playing on the game system and she took up reading and the TV never went on. She got a job a few months later and was able to catch up on her credit card payments and miraculously everything went back to normal. She noticed her kids playing more, or they were watching movies together again and she had gone back to her two favorite shows that she watched every week. She told me that she hadn't noticed this change of habit until after she got her credit card current. That's when she realized that when she wasn't making payments on the entertainment center, it was almost like she no longer owned it—like it wasn't hers to use.

Just like the children I mentioned in Chapter One—the ones who get tons of free toys and break them because they don't feel like them earned them—you can get that same feeling at any age if you're not paying for things or at least doing something for those things. Even a credit card payment doesn't make an item yours--not until it's paid in full.

Case in point: In most states lenders won't repossess your TV for late payments, but a car or a house? YOU BET. Those notes are owned by banks, and they'll leave you homeless or car-less if you don't pay them.

Recently a friend of mine had her car repossessed. She was behind only $82 and was 35 days late. I called the company to try to help her because they refused to reinstate the payment arrangement with her. They wanted the full balance on the loan. This was her second run-in with that company. About 11 months prior to this, she was behind $200 and about 45 days late. She was having financial difficulties because of days off work due to being hospitalized. In the end the bank refused to do anything about it and told her that they would sell the car at auction if she didn't pay the loan in full. She had paid on the account for over four years already and had never been late except for those two times.

When I intervened they suggested that I loan her the money to pay it off in full. They refused to do anything but take the full amount. I had her send a letter to the president of the company pleading hardship and to have them take another look at her payment history. Still they refused to budge. Finally she had to borrow money from her employer and friends to come up with the full amount. She was never a credit risk in the past and now had some legitimate hardships.   The bank didn't care that she was having problems. <u>They just didn't care</u>. She had paid over 80 percent of her loan by that point and still the car didn't belong to her. She didn't really own it.

So with these examples you can see that by using bank loans or credit cards to buy stuff, you don't actually OWN that stuff—until you've paid it all off <u>in full</u>. How can you keep from falling into the false ownership trap? Work out a way to pay <u>cash</u>. Don't listen to the hype of advertisers who try to tell you that you have to have things now, on easy credit, when in reality, YOU DON'T.

CHAPTER

Building Your New Dream

Based on New Beliefs

Where do you find truth? Well, let's look at where you keep your eyes and ears tuned throughout much of the day—the media. Magazines, movies, and "so-called" Reality TV tell us about Martians, break-ups, and things that aren't true. After getting depressed by watching the news, the TV ads come on to show us that some little pill will make everything better, and to remind us that pretty much everything we eat is bad for us.

So what do we believe? If I believed everything that I was told about food, I would be starving to death and not be able to eat anything at all. If I took all the drugs that I was told to take because of things that were going on in my life and with my body, I would be taking 100 pills a day. If I believed everything that I was told, then I wouldn't have my own mind or my own opinion. I would be a robot, thinking the way "they" tell me to think and I wouldn't be myself.

Is that the way I want to live? Of course not. I want to be free to live my own life and *DO* what I want to do and make up my own mind about things and not let anyone else influence me. After all, this is America, and in America we're supposed to be free from control and persecution, to live our lives as free people. Isn't that what it's all about? Isn't that why we're here? To be ourselves and not be told what to do by others? That's why I'm here. I want to think for myself and make my own decisions—that's what I want. Freedom of choice is a big part of my American Dream.

Life, Liberty and the Pursuit of Happiness

So if we want to be free and independent people, but we've been working our butts off to get that money to buy stuff that's supposed to make us happy (that plan isn't working), then let's go back to the Declaration of Independence for some guidance on how we can dig ourselves out of this debt hole and get back to making our dreams come true.

If you look back at the times when you were truly happy—what were the common elements? Was it that paycheck, or was it when you actually got something accomplished at work? Was it that big-screen TV, or was it playing a game on it with your kids where you laughed and howled for hours? Was it about that fast car, or was it taking it to the beach or mountains with family and friends and enjoying time together?

If you start taking account of your life, I think you'll find that money is just something you use to help achieve a dream; money isn't the goal. And in some cases, money isn't needed at all. A sunset enjoyed together is absolutely free. Throwing a stick for the dog to fetch has no late fee attached to it. Cleaning up your local park with the Boy or Girl Scouts doesn't earn you a dime, but it sure feels good, doesn't it? To me, these descriptions are about the pursuit of happiness-- the chase, and then the accomplishment of each goal that you make.

Change Your Mind

Yes, you have to have money to survive, this is true, but what about being <u>happy</u> about all of the <u>other</u> things in life? Wouldn't that be a switch in viewpoint? The truth is that if you go into your day pursuing <u>happiness</u>, instead of pursuing <u>money</u>, some very wonderful things can occur. When you do the things that feel right to you—go to the gym, spend time with your family, have fun at your job, do community projects—you start to feel <u>rich</u>. Fulfilled. Whether you save an animal, plant a tree, become more active in your church, or get the city to finally fill in that nasty pothole in the middle of your road—you're being productive in your world. You're not just working to try to make money to pay the bills.

Being productive is important for everybody, including your retired father. Have you ever known someone who retired from their job after 50 years and then within a very short time, they died or got extremely ill? One theory says it's because their production for all those years was high, and then all of a sudden they didn't have anything to do so they sat in front of the TV and

STOPPED producing. I agree with that theory. Retirees who have a plan for what they're going to do—whether it's a hobby such as building furniture, golfing every day, or doing community work—are more likely to continue to be happy and live full lives, rich lives. But people who sit in front of TVs and don't have anything to do or produce will inevitably lose their vitality and motivation towards life.

Redefining Ourselves and Our Worth

So does happiness really exist or is it all just a big lie? I believe that happiness exists inside of all of us, not because we have a bunch of stuff but because we are being exactly who we want to *BE*. It's who we are that counts and what we're doing that brings about ultimate happiness. To feel happiness I believe that a person must make sure he has integrity, no matter what the situation. The definition of integrity is: "*Adherence to moral and ethical principles; soundness of moral character; honesty.*"

If you can maintain your integrity and be ethical, moral and honest with yourself and others, you can do exactly what you want to do that produces the product that you are looking for. By using those values as your foundation, you can pursue and reach your goals to be happy. And by doing so, you will influence others to do the same.

You see, in *BEING* the person you want to *BE*, you become more willing to expand into other areas of your environment and begin *DOING* more things, which leads to *HAVING* more happiness and a feeling of <u>worth</u>. We're talking about personal worth, not the "I've got a lot of stuff" worth. Even if you don't get paid for cleaning up the park or fixing that pothole in the street, just the satisfaction of doing it makes you happier in the long run. Don't you think?

So before we tackle your debt and how to handle it, let's have you take stock of your PERSONAL WORTH. What are some of the things that are important to you personally, the things that you value?

_____

_____

_____

_____

_____

_____

_____

_____

_____

_____

_____

_____

_____

_____

_____

_____

Keep this list nearby as you make decisions about how to handle your finances—what work you'll do to make money, the actions you're going to do to reduce your debt, and how and what you'll spend money on in the future. Keep your personal values and your personal worth in mind. It should make your future choices a little easier.

CHAPTER 10

Tools to Rebalance Your Life

Congratulations! You've already used the first tool to rebalance your life. Yes, that's right. You've already started making a change. You've listed your PERSONAL WORTH—what's important to you personally—which is the foundation of your values and integrity. It'll help you stay clear on who you want to *BE*. In a moment we'll start putting together that plan of what you have to *DO* to reach your full potential, and your goal to *HAVE* those things that bring true happiness.

Remember, creating a real American Dream starts with *BE*, then *DO*, then *HAVE*. So put away that credit card. You've already been "doing" too much with that anyway.

The reason I've been talking about your personal worth and achieving happiness through a productive environment is to offer an alternative to what you're facing now. You can spend all of your time at work to be able to buy that new entertainment system that you want, but because you spend all that time at work, you don't get to use it very often. You're too tired. You can get a loan to buy that beautiful new car, but it might sit in the parking lot during your long hours at work, so you never get to go anywhere, except deeper in debt.

> **If your life feels out of balance or out of control, you're not alone.**

I'm not saying that you did everything wrong. What I'm saying is that you didn't have the <u>tools</u> regarding finances to be able to <u>change</u> what you were doing. In most cases, nobody taught you how to handle this thing called money or debt, so you just went off and did the best that you could.

So you created this situation. It's not going to change overnight. There are things that you have to *DO* and steps that you have to take in order to change the life that you've created for yourself. It's not impossible; you can do it if you DECIDE to do it. It's as simple as that.

You might think, "yeah, but really, if I just had 20 percent more money, or if I just hit that jackpot, all my money problems would be solved." NOPE. People all over the income map suffer from the same problem--not having the tools to handle money. Seriously, for most people, the more money they make, the more they spend. It doesn't matter what their income is. A millionaire can make one million dollars and spend two million.

Let's say you've been living for a couple of years with an annual income of $50,000 without any problem. Then you get a raise and make $60,000 and all of a sudden you're spending that amount or more. You immediately get letters from banks telling you that your credit limit has been raised. Yahoo! Spend more than you make!

I was talking to a man the other day who told me that at one point he was making $60,000 per month in a sales company, and then all of a sudden his income dropped to $16,000 per month. Before his income dipped he was spending every dime and had nothing in savings to show for it. NOTHING. He told me that he was practically destitute when his income dropped. It took him months and a lot of talking to creditors to handle his situation. He learned very quickly that having a lot of money didn't bring happiness—just more debt. If he had the tools then that he has now, he could have handled that drop in income with no debt or worries, and would still have been able to reach his goals.

The Key to Reaching Your Goals

Have you ever made a New Year's resolution like losing weight or quitting smoking and have it last about a day and a half? Did you fail because it was too hard? Or you just couldn't stick with it? If so, more than likely you failed to achieve your goal because you didn't have a good plan.

I've made too many New Year's resolutions where I wanted to lose 20 pounds by a certain date, but never had any plan that would accomplish it. So I would start out on the first of January thinking I was going to lose weight, but I didn't do anything to change my eating habits, and I didn't do any research on what would be good for my body. My New Years "diets" would never last and I would get frustrated and feel bad for not being able to stick with it. It was because I didn't fully do my homework, know exactly what I was going to do, put a plan together that I agreed with and stick to it. If I would have done those things, I would have been able to accomplish my goals. I would have had what I wanted.

It's the same with finances. You need to see the entire picture--how much money you have, how much debt you have, your Action Plan to reduce that debt, your method of sticking to that Action Plan, and your program to set and reach goals that are obtainable.

This understanding of the entire picture is the key. It'll be the most powerful tool you have in achieving your goals in life, no matter what they are, because any goal can be achieved by doing these simple steps. That's right. You will be able to apply these powerful tools to every part of your life, not just your finances. You will be that person you always wanted to be, without other people's influences.

To build your American Dream, we'll use the Personal Worth List as your foundation (because that includes your personal values and integrity), have you select who you want to *BE*, then put together the Action Plan of what you have to *DO* to get there. And when you've successfully accomplished those goals, we'll celebrate the fact that you *HAVE* the things you want in life. Sound good to you?

So let's get going on the road to financial freedom, your American Dream, and understanding what you can do to bring yourself all of the happiness that you deserve.

CHAPTER 11

Be the Person YOU Want to Be

Let's start this process by finding out *WHO YOU REALLY ARE*. Do you have any idea? Look at what you do for a living and ask yourself, "Is this what I want to do for the rest of my life?" Be honest with yourself. Do you want to do something else but don't feel like you can get there? Do you have a plan so that you can achieve your goal? Do you want to be a business owner or a cashier in a hamburger joint? The choice is yours.

These are questions you have to answer for yourself. But first, sit down and take a good look at your life and who YOU really are. Are you a mother, a husband, a grandmother, an aunt, a friend, a waitress, a teacher, a truck driver, a volunteer? You probably have many labels, titles, or jobs, because you can *BE* many things. Take this time to write down all of the things that you are.

I AM

_____

_____

_____

_____

_____

_____

_____

_____

_____

Now put down all of the things that you are <u>because</u> <u>somebody else told you that you had to be that thing</u>. Let's say your mother told you that you should be a lawyer and it's what she wanted for you, but not necessarily what you wanted. Or say that the doctor told you that you had some mental disorder, something that you "are" but you did NOT agree to. Write all of these things down.

I AM BECAUSE OF SOMEONE / SOMETHING ELSE

What did you find? How many of the things that you essentially "are" turned out to be things that you actually wanted to be or agreed to be, versus what someone else wanted you to be? That's eye opening isn't it?

Now, let's rearrange the two lists based upon your own decisions right now. For instance, if you hated being a nurse because you were pushed into going to medical school by your father, can you put that aside and determine if you actually like being a nurse now, because you help people, or because it's for the right cause? Or do you really want to be a chef?

Can you move this item over to the other list so that you're in agreement with it, because today it's <u>your</u> decision and not someone else's?   Whatever your decision, it will be the right one because it's yours.

Let's say you're a niece and your father tells you that you have to be nice to your Uncle Joe, but you've always hated Uncle Joe and hated being a niece. Instead of hating to be that thing, what about finding the good points in Uncle Joe and focusing on them so that you can be a niece and be happy about it? It's what you agree with *BEING* that makes all of the difference in the world.

Any time you're *BEING* someone or something that is not of your own choosing and you feel like you're out of control in your life, you can end up hating yourself or what you're doing. I mean, let's face it—it would be hard to be a carpenter and do carpentry and be good at it if you didn't <u>want</u> to do it in the first place. This writing process is about regaining control of your life by making your own decisions about who you really are.

Play with these two lists, move things back and forth. Who are you? Who are you because of someone else's dreams? Which roles are OKAY now, because you have, on this day and in this place, agreed that they ARE OKAY?

Now that you've straightened out the two lists, take another look at them. Are there things that you "are" that you still disagree with? If this is the case then it's time to determine if you can get rid of them or not. If some "jobs" or "titles" will take longer to leave, then put together a plan to move them off of your list.

WHY am I having you spend so much time on this identity list? Because as you reach for your new dream, you can't just drop all of the things you are currently *BEING*, without an Action Plan. So figure out what you can live with for awhile and what you want to *BE* that brings you the income you need to handle your debt while you start building towards your new dream.

For instance, let's say you hate being a waitress, but you need the money. You can't lose the waitress income—yet. Well, what do you <u>want</u> to *BE* instead? If you really want to *BE* a beautician, you've got to put together a plan to make that happen. You need to keep being a waitress until you can make that new dream come true.

Do your research—find out what it will cost to go to school to learn the trade, or if you can get scholarships or make payments, and what sort of a time commitment is involved? Search for reputable schools, see if they have any placement or internship programs to help you get a job when you're finished. Look at the cost of a license and how and where you might start into business once you're finished with beautician school.

When you have all of the data, you can write out a plan on how to do it, setting targets with dates for when you'll have each step completed. But remember something that's very important about this process, don't STOP doing these things to achieve your goals because of money. If you do need money to go to school, find out about scholarships, tell people you're going to go to school, start doing research online, go to the library and get books. But NEVER stop yourself because of money. Do something to *BE* that person that you want to be, despite all odds. Be creative and never stop moving forward on it.

Let's say that you need $1,000 to start a class. Look at your current finances and find out how much you can put away each week to pay for your tuition. If you can set aside $100 per week from your waitress income for this new dream, make a goal of having your $1,000 in ten weeks. Then find out when the next classes start and target out for that. In the mean time, do all of those other things to prepare yourself for your new career. And by all means, MAKE MORE MONEY! As a waitress you can make tips, so make more of them. Work faster and smarter and be happy! By working towards what you want, you'll be happier. It's what happens with people who are on their own path and moving towards their own American Dream!

Lets recap. It all starts with you agreeing to continue *BEING* a waitress while you start acting like you're

BEING a beautician—the old and the new—so you can *DO* your current job while you're *DOING* the studies to take you to your new goal, to *HAVE* the new career. Get it?

Think this sounds crazy, this *BEING* thing? Look back at your life. Any time you wanted something, didn't you start by creating that finished picture <u>in your mind</u>, where you were being the new thing? You "dreamed" of being the graduate, the new car owner, the newlywed, the most valuable player. You SAW what you wanted in your mind and pushed towards it. Now you're going to learn to do that by consciously making a DECISION to *DO* it. It won't be done by accident.

12 CHAPTER

Creating Your New Dream

Now that you've listed all of the things you were in the past, let's give you the opportunity to start creating the New You. Remember, we start with *BE*, and then we'll fill in the Action Plan--the *DO*, so that you can *HAVE*. I know, I know, how many more times am I going to say this? As many as it takes so it's drilled into your brain!

Your Goals—Not Somebody Else's

Here's the deal—they are <u>your</u> goals, purposes and dreams and not anybody else's. Yours and yours alone. You can talk to people to decide how you're going to do something or ask for help in certain areas, but don't let them sway you. Look at all the facts before you make your decision and *DO* the work. Don't let someone else do all the research on something for you because then it won't be your dream, it'll be somebody else's.

Of course your life is connected to others—a spouse, kids, or other friends or family members--you should have agreement from them for their help. For instance, if you need to go to night school for 12 weeks, you'll need agreement from your spouse to either watch the kids or get a sitter. When you ask for their agreement, be enthusiastic about it. It's what you want and you need their help. Most people want to help.

Don't Jeopardize Your Own Integrity

Remember that setting and accomplishing your goals works best when you maintain your integrity. I can't stress this point enough. Be honest with yourself and don't lose sight of your own Personal Worth, just because of the desires or needs of others. I know adult children who are still so dependent on their parents that they don't do what they want to do because they're still trying to please their parents and do what their parents want. This is why this exercise is so important, because sometimes we look past what we want to do and instead follow the lead or influence of others. So in the end we're not being the person we want to be.

Take Responsibility for Your Own Life

You can take opinions from other people, but ultimately the life you create is your decision and yours alone. By taking responsibility for your own life, you're also taking responsibility for others' lives because you're showing them that you are determined to do something and you do it.

"Responsibility" is not defined as *blame or regret*, as so many people think. In the *World English Dictionary*, definition number three states that responsibility is: *"The ability or authority to act or decide on one's own, without supervision."*

When you're "responsible," you have the ability to make decisions on your own.

I can remember when I was 23 years old and had two kids. My mother lived in another state and I talked to her several times a week on the phone. She had a lot of control over me and my decisions, or so I thought. (In actuality, I gave her that control over me). One morning

I wanted to go to the beach. I love the beach and hadn't been there in a few years. For a fleeting moment I actually thought about calling my mother to get permission, and then I realized how absurd that was! I had put so much of my life into her hands that even though she was 600 miles away, I didn't think I could do even the simplest thing—like go to the beach—without first getting her approval.

When I recognized that dependency pattern and stopped it that day, I felt like I grew up. I disconnected myself from thinking that I had to get permission to do things, and I started making decisions for myself. I packed up the kids and we went to the beach and it felt great! It's those silly little things in life that sometimes trap us into doing things that we're not even aware we're doing. That day I started thinking for myself and doing what I wanted to do. You would think that a woman at age 23 with two kids of her own would be making her own decisions in life. But looking back on it now, I realize that I was putting most of my decision-making on my mother. I was not taking full responsibility for my own life. If my mother told me to do something, and I did it and something bad happened or I didn't like it, I could and would blame her, even though it was me who actually did it. So in some cases it's easier to take orders or opinions from others and use them, because if they're wrong or it doesn't work out then it's *not your fault* but rather the fault of the person who told you to do it in the first place. Do you see how that goes? As an adult you're still giving that ultimate responsibility to your parents, or your spouse, or someone else. Another example would be a parent wanting you to go to college and you go. It's not what you want to do. And when you're in college you party, get Fs, and never have any intention of getting through it in the first place. You flunk out of school, and whose fault is it? Well in a lot of cases, students blame their parents for this because it was their parents who told them to do it in the first place. And when it didn't work out, that person doesn't take responsibility himself for flunking out.

On the other hand, if that person <u>wanted</u> to go to college and was determined to get through on his own, then there is a very good possibility that he will do well because it's his purpose, his goal, and his <u>responsibility</u> to get through it.

Write them Down

Now that you've decided to create your own dream based on your own decisions, and you're doing it with integrity and being responsible for your own life, let's start building that new world that you want. Based upon your Personal Worth List, what is <u>your</u> new American Dream? You can have several-- short-term, long-term, to be done tomorrow or next year--it doesn't matter. Make them as specific as possible. Do you want to lose weight (how much), find a new job (what type), meet the RIGHT person for a change (list the values they need to have), or get totally out of debt (how much and when)? Do you want to become a mechanic, a painter, a teacher or a multi-level marketer? Do you want to sing, dance or wash dogs? Do you want to be a millionaire, own a house or find your long lost brother-in-law? Whatever they are list them on the following page.

MY NEW AMERICAN DREAM

Are you having trouble with the list? As you start to write something down, is there a voice or a thought that pops up and says, "Oh you'll NEVER be able to *DO* that." Well, you've just hit one of the mental roadblocks, installed by family, society, or some earlier experience

you had. Just ignore that voice or silence it and KEEP
WRITING.

_____

_____

_____

_____

_____

_____

_____

_____

_____

_____

_____

_____

_____

DO this exercise honestly and thoroughly. But remember that just naming your goals or dreams isn't enough. The next step will be to put a plan together to achieve them--a step-by-step plan that you can do to achieve your goals.

If you're 50 years old and you want to be an NBA star, is that doable? Not in this life. So don't set a goal that's so impossible for you to reach that you fail before you even start. Be realistic in your goals, be honest with yourself and what you really want to *BE,* and remember that in order to *BE* that thing, you're going to have to work for it by *DOING* something to achieve it.

This includes facing your finances and getting them straightened out. Here's where you learn to face the music. Get ready. But don't worry—you're not facing it alone.

CHAPTER

Reaching Your Goals:

The Action Plan

Now that you've written down what you want to *BE* in life, the next step is the process of *DOING* those things that will get you to that goal.

Did you ever gaze with envy at someone who was living their dream? Their life looks so <u>easy</u>. What you don't see is all the hard work it took for them to get there, including writing down the details of their Action Plan and then *DOING* every step.

Take Tom Hanks, who had to lose a LOT of weight for the movie *Philadelphia* and again for *Castaway*. How about the movie *Titanic*—the actors had to be in those freezing waters for hours while filming. When you saw their blue lips on film, it wasn't makeup.

Now let's look at a professional football or basketball player. Pro athletes work incredibly hard to achieve their goals. That includes drilling and exercising every single day, handling injuries, competing at the highest level, spending long hours on planes away from their families, and much more. All YOU see is the result—the big paycheck and the fun lifestyle. But behind that ideal scene that they are living are these crucial elements: A GOAL, A PLAN AND HARD WORK.

Because they are *BEING* exactly who they want to *BE*, they *DO* exactly what it takes to *HAVE* the life they want. How many times did Michael Jordon retire from basketball, or Barbra Streisand step away from doing concerts? They just kept *DOING* it because they loved it and it was who they were.

Let's Get Productive

It's time to get productive and *DO* those things that will make you who you really want to *BE* and in turn to have that life that you've decided to *HAVE*. The first thing to *DO* is to decide that you're going to *BE* in control of your finances. We'll handle the rest of your goals a little later, because right now we need to get that financial "problem" out of the way so that you can put your Action Plan together to achieve the rest of your goals.

Chances are that up until now you've not actually decided to *BE* in control of your finances, but have allowed your finances to control you. So the first thing to *DO* here is to make sure that you decide to *BE* someone who wants to be in control of their finances. Have you done that? Great! Add that to your Goals List.

Now, what are the things that you have to *DO* in order to get this part of your life under control? It begins with you taking an honest look at where you are right now and where you want to go.

Look at the current picture? YIKES! That's right. Reaching those new goals depends upon you CONFRONTING that picture of where you are now and putting together a realistic, step-by-step plan for reaching your goal. For example, if you want your weight to be 150 pounds and you're now at 200 pounds, that's the current picture. If you want to be out of debt and right now you owe $35,000 on your credit cards, that's the current picture.

Whether you want a different career, a healthier body, or a new house, it'll be a lot easier to put your plan together if you don't have the money problem in the way. You have to find out exactly how much debt you have and design a plan to trim it, weekly. It's not impossible. People work this plan every day. It's all about choices.

Smart Math: Choices

If you think back to how you got into debt in the first place, it was really about <u>choices</u>. So let's use an example or two on how to make better spending choices to reach your goals faster.

If you rent an apartment for $1,000 per month and get a roommate, then your share is $500, which is pretty reasonable. You probably have to pay a deposit to move in, maybe another $1,000 which you and your roommate split. If you need furniture, a refrigerator, a bedroom set, and other household essentials and you buy them <u>used</u>, you might look at paying about $1,000 for the lot, and in most cases you'll split this with your roommate. So if you're paying cash for all of this, your out-of-pocket expense is about $1,500 to move in, with no additional bills except your monthly living expenses.

However, if you use a credit card and get all of that furniture new, you could easily pay about $5,000. Of course you and your roommate will split it, but if the card is in your name only, you'll have to depend on that person to pay their part of the debt and be with you for years to do it. Your minimum monthly payments on the card will be about $230. This seems easy, your roommate will pay for half of it, and you will get everything that you want. But with you making only the minimum payment each month, depending on the interest rate it might take you 20 or 30 years to pay for that furniture. Unless you actually keep that roommate forever, you'll end up with this debt all by yourself.

Think about it. This $5,000 bill will grow and grow because of the credit card interest, and your roommate, in most cases will only pay back half of the furniture amount without interest. So now you're stuck with thousands of dollars of debt that you'll have to pay on for years. What happens when your roommate decides to move out because she gets a new job elsewhere or she's getting married? You may even lose a friend because you're stuck holding those bills and you blame her for it.

So what are your options in this scenario? Maybe you could get that used furniture to start with, and then when you're set up in the new place and want something new, save for it and pay cash. You and your roommate could put money aside every week. Once you have the money and have bought the new item, put the old item up for sale and recoup some of your money. This way you're getting something back and getting that item that you wanted. And best of all you're not making credit card payments and paying those huge interest payments.

Here's another way to go: Take one of those offers that give you free interest for a year. I've seen furniture stores do this in the past. They offer "12 months same as cash," which means that if you buy a living room set that costs $1,200 today, it'll still be $1,200 in 364 days, with no added interest. So do the math and divide the $1,200 by 12 which equals $100 per month. Can you afford that? Before you buy you need to make sure that you can and will make that monthly payment like clockwork. If you go over the 12 months and haven't paid it all off, the store will bill you for ALL of the accumulated interest that would have been charged throughout the entire year, usually at a rate of 18 to 29 percent. Then you're in the same boat of piling up credit debt, where you keep paying on the account forever. But if you use the "12 months same as cash" deal, and actually pay the bill off within 12 months, you're getting what you want and still living within your means. It's a win-win situation. CHOICES.

CHAPTER 14

You, The Debt Detective

This program will help you face and handle your money situations so that you can achieve your American Dream. It is a step-by-step process which will include these actions:

1. Total up ALL of your debt from every source.

2. List ALL expenses—everything from monthly rent and annual vehicle registration, to vacations and Christmas spending.

3. Calculate ALL of your spending, and break it down into a weekly number.

4. Add up every source of income you can think of.

5. Design a BUDGET to help you manage your spending so you can better handle your weekly, monthly, and yearly bills.

6. Create your new American Dream plan, using the Budget and Goals.

The first step in handling your debt is to find out how much debt you actually have, and how much more you run up each month with charges, interest, and late fees. But where do you gather that information? Here's where you become a detective, hunting down all the details to solve your own Credit Scene Investigation.

Understanding Your Credit Cards

What do you do when you receive your credit card statement? Do you study it intently, reading all of the fine print? Or do you rip off the return portion that only includes the "minimum payment" amount, and write a check for that amount? Most people never look at the balance due, the interest rate, or the amount of time it will take to pay off the debt. If you pay online a similar thing occurs. In most cases, the payment choice defaults to the minimum payment and makes it somewhat inconvenient for you to pay more.

At this point you're going to study the front and back of that bill to help you get a better understanding of your credit cards and to figure out <u>realistically</u> what it'll take to pay them off. But before we begin there's one word on the bill that we need to define. It's called **APR**, which stands for Annual Percentage Rate. This, essentially, is the interest rate you're being charged for borrowing money from a credit card company. Many credit cards have separate APRs listed for each type of money borrowing system—balance transfers, cash advances or other low-interest offers, so you want to make sure you find the correct APR.

Let's start by having you look over <u>one</u> of your statements, a current one, preferably less than 30 days old. Find each of these items on your own statement and circle them or highlight them with a marker.

1. Creditor – the name of the credit card company.

2. Balance – your current total balance, including interest, fees, etc.

3. APR/Interest Rate – there may be different interest rates (APRs) for different things on your bill:

   a. Interest rate on charges
   b. Interest rate on cash advances
   c. Interest rate on balance transfers

4. Minimum Payment – the lowest dollar amount you can pay each month.

The credit card companies are now required by law (under the Credit Card Accountability, Responsibility, and Disclosure Act) to show you how many years it will take to pay off your debt if all you make is the minimum payment each month. That calculation is designed to give you a clear picture of all of those fees you're paying, and how they add a lot more time and money for you to finally be debt-free. Look for that information on your bill as well. If it's not on your statement, search the bank or credit card company website. Search your bill for this info and highlight it.

5. Years to Payoff – how long it will take to pay it off, making only the minimum monthly payment.

6. Total Payoff Estimate – the total amount of money that you'll end up paying including interest and fees by only making the minimums or your current level of monthly payment.

You may be shocked to see what you've gotten yourself into with these credit card companies!

Okay, did you find all of these items on your statement? Congratulations! You're officially a Debt Detective. Now you're about to solve the mystery of where all of your hard-earned money has gone. READY? Don't panic—just take each action, one step at a time.

STEP 1. *GATHER <u>ALL</u> OF YOUR STATEMENTS.* As I said, your statements should be less than 30 days old. If not, then use what you have so that you don't stop moving forward in the book. If you can't find your statements, go online and either print out your latest bill from the company website or get a separate piece of paper where you can write down the information necessary to complete the next step.

STEP 2. *GET A CALCULATOR.* Don't worry—you don't have to be a math wizard. This is pretty basic stuff you're about to do. If you don't have a calculator you can use your iPhone or computer calculator.

STEP 3. *FIND THE INTEREST RATE (APR) YOU'RE BEING CHARGED.* If the credit card company is doing their job it should be on your statement. If you still can't see it on your statement, you may need to go online or call your credit card company who must provide this information to you. If there are several APRs listed— for balance transfer, cash advances, etc., list them all.

STEP 4. WRITE DOWN THE INFORMATION FOR EACH CARD. Fill out the Credit Card Debt worksheet on the next page with all of the information you've gathered from your credit card statements. For example, see below:

CREDITOR	BALANCE	INTEREST RATE (APR)	YEARS TO PAYOFF	TOTAL PAYOFF ESTIMATE	MINIMUM PAYMENTS
ABC VISA	$ 2896.23	24.99 %	5 Years	$4608.85	$96.01

Note: You can also download the financial spreadsheet from my website at www.thedebtlady.com

Credit Card Debt Worksheet

	CREDITOR	A BALANCE	INTEREST	B YEARS TO PAYOFF	C TOTAL PAYOFF ESTIMATE	MINIMUM PAYMENTS
1.		$	%		$	$
2.		$	%		$	$
3.		$	%		$	$
4.		$	%		$	$
5.		$	%		$	$
6.		$	%		$	$
7.		$	%		$	$
8.		$	%		$	$
9.		$	%		$	$
10.		$	%		$	$
11.		$	%		$	$
12.		$	%		$	$
13.		$	%		$	$
14.		$	%		$	$
15.		$	%		$	$
16.		$	%		$	$
17.		$	%		$	$
	TOTAL	$			$	$

STEP 5. ADD UP YOUR TOTALS. Remember how I told you to grab a calculator? Now is the time to use it. We're going to play a game. But you have to promise not to cheat! How can I cheat, you ask? The rule is, you have to follow the three steps below without reading anything further. Agreed? Good! As you may have noticed on the previous page I labeled three columns (A) (B) and (C). Here's what I want you to do:

- *Total up all of your balances in Column (A) and write down the total in the box below that says (A).*

- *Take the largest number in Column (B) and write it in the box below that says (B).*

- *Total up everything in Column (C) and write it in the box below that says (C).*

Great Job! Now you can read each column description!

A	B	C
$	Years	$
This is the total debt that you actually owe at this time.	If you continue making your minimum payments on all your cards, this is how many years it will take you to pay them all off.	This is how much you will ACTUALLY end up paying if you continue making minimum payments including interest.

Shocking isn't it? Are you ready for an even BIGGER shock?

Subtract Column (A) from Column (C) to see how much you'll end up spending <u>just in interest</u>. Okay now pick yourself up off the floor and actually write that number down. Total interest cost for ALL of your credit card debt is:

$$\boxed{\$ \qquad\qquad\qquad\qquad\qquad\qquad}$$

Wow! This doesn't even seem legal does it? You'll end up spending that much more money—all because you bought something that you knew you couldn't afford in the first place because you had to use credit to buy it.

IMPORTANT NOTE: Every time you charge on a card, you extend the amount of time that you'll be paying it. So, the above exercise only applies if you STOP using your credit cards...NOW!

I want you to close your eyes and imagine something that you purchased with one of your cards. For example, a television set. Write down the name of that item:

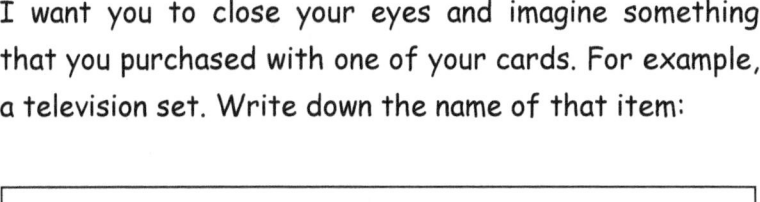

Now, did you actually NEED that item? Or was it something that you WANTED? If you said it was an item that you NEEDED, well I can understand. Sometimes you need credit cards for emergency purchases or car repairs. But, if you said it was something you WANTED, and you couldn't actually afford it in the first place, then you need to re-evaluate your spending habits and make some changes.

Here's the scary part about borrowing money, which is what you're doing when you charge something on a credit card. By the time you pay off that loan, that item may have depreciated in value or even stopped working. Chances are it's been in the garage or the city dump for years before the money that you borrowed to buy it is finally paid off.

The Deadly Receipt

"Do you want your receipt?" That's what cashiers are asking now days. They say it saves trees if they don't have to print out those paper receipts. Besides, you don't <u>really</u> want to know how much you're spending, right? You can now swipe your credit card almost anywhere—without ever signing for the purchases you make.

If you stop and LOOK at the bottom of that receipt where you have to sign, there is a statement underneath which says: "Customer agrees to pay the above total amount according to the cardholders agreement." So when you sign that credit card receipt it means <u>you agreed to pay</u>. But these days with the "swipe and no receipt" game, maybe you'll forget how much you spend. So, how are you going to keep track of your spending if you don't have any bills or receipts to hold in your hand? *Good question.*

The credit card companies and banks have made it easy for you to avoid confronting your debt. Same pitch—

"Save trees! Go Green! Get your credit card/bank statement online!" Since they don't show up in the mailbox anymore, do you pay attention to them? Probably not. This is the time to change all that.

The Real Price for a Credit Card

Let's say that a salesperson at an electronics shop approached you after noticing you staring at that beautiful Blu-ray, Plasma, HD, blah blah television set the size of your front door. Ooohh! And he told you that the television was *only* $800. Well, maybe to him! But you sure don't have $800 just sitting in your pocket. So you tell the salesman, "Sorry, not today. I don't have 800 bucks." But wait! He then tells you that he can give you the TV today, NO MONEY DOWN, just monthly payments. But in reality, you're agreeing to buy that $800 TV for $1300 or more because of the interest that's going to be tacked on over the course of the repayment plan. Doesn't seem fair does it?

It's the same when you buy a car and take out a loan. That shiny new car or truck might have a sticker price of $25,000 but when you agree to pay it over six years, the interest and fees make the final price of that car $35,000 or MORE. But you have "low monthly payments," right? Yeah, that's sneaky. As a side note on buying a car, it's very difficult to come up with the cash to buy a car outright these days. So something that you can do is make weekly payments to your car company. Even though you have a five- or six-year loan with them, and the interest is exorbitant, making weekly payments will pay that loan off faster because your principle goes down every week. It saves you big bucks in the long run. So for those big purchases, the more payments you make a month, the faster the debt will be paid!

The problem with credit cards is that people don't actually realize how much money they'll end up spending for something that they just bought. They think they're purchasing that item based off of the sticker price like with a car or house. But in reality if they're buying it with a credit card they're spending a lot more than they bargained for. With credit cards, you can continue to charge; literally for life. That $5,000 charge that you made when you were 21 years old to get into that new apartment stays with you throughout your lifetime, well into retirement, if you're only making minimum payments on that card.

By taking the time to figure out how much you're <u>actually paying</u> to use your credit cards, I'm hoping you'll reconsider each purchase and become more careful with your money.

So we can agree after doing that little exercise about interest rates and minimum payments that you obviously don't want to spend all your hard-earned money on credit card bills every month. Right? Well, you're in luck! I'm going to give you some tips that will help you **save money**.

Tip #1: Cut Your Credit Card Interest Rate

The first thing we need to do is look at all of that interest you're paying. I want you to go back to the exercise we did earlier and find the card with the highest interest rate. Now re-write it here:

CREDITOR	BALANCE	INTEREST RATE (APR)	YEARS TO PAYOFF	TOTAL PAYOFF ESTIMATE	MINIMUM PAYMENTS
	$	%		$	$

Looks to me like you're throwing away possibly hundreds of dollars towards this card. Agreed? The first thing we need to do is bring down that interest. This can be done in six easy steps.

I know what you're thinking: "Yeah, I'll just call them." Yes, you can. But the hardest part is picking up the phone, and from my experience, most people have a hard time with it. They say they'll do it tomorrow or maybe a week from now. I'm asking you to humor me for one second and actually follow these six steps right here, right now! And every time you finish a step, I want you to initial your name and date on the line below that step, showing you've completed that action. Let's begin.

STEP 1. Find your statement for that high-interest rate card.

_____   _____
         Initial   Date

STEP 2. Find your credit card account number on the statement.

_____   _____
　　　　Initial　　　　　　　　　　　　Date

STEP 3. Find the credit card company telephone number.

Tel:

STEP 4. Call the credit card company.

_____   _____
　　　　Initial　　　　　　　　　　　　Date

STEP 5. Request the following information and write it down:

INTEREST RATE BEING CHARGED NOW	%
INTEREST RATE BEING CHARGED IF IN DEFAULT	%

STEP 6. Request nicely that they lower your interest rate.

_____   _____
　　　　Initial　　　　　　　　　　　　Date

IMPORTANT

If you're stuck on this step because the credit card company won't lower your interest rate, here are some helpful tools!

#1 - Know what the average credit card interest rate is by going online and doing research on that credit card company. Find out what they're offering new customers now and see if there are any "specials" going on. That way you have some leverage. When you find their new/special interest rate, suggest a lower rate for you as well, and try and keep it within the same range. Asking for an interest rate of one percent isn't realistic.

#2 - If the person on the phone won't work with you, hang up and call right back to see if you can get a different representative.

#3 - Request to speak to a manager or supervisor. Most managers have more authority to make necessary changes in order to keep their customers happy.

#4 - Let them know that you may close the account and find another credit card provider with better terms.

#5 - Explain to them that you're experiencing a financial hardship and that you have a total of $_____ in debt that you are trying to pay off. (If you do this step, make sure that you actually <u>do</u> have a hardship; don't ever lie!)

#6 - Try another time! If they're reluctant to change your rate at this time, call back later or earlier in the day. Banks change their policies all the time. Try calling in a few weeks and see if that helps. Persistence is key.

The reason this five-minute phone call is so important is because it really can make a world of difference in how much you spend!

Here is an easy example of how much money you could be saving from interest alone:

Credit Card "A"		Credit Card "B"
Balance: $10,000		Balance: $10,000
Interest Rate (24.99%)	←Compare→	Interest Rate (10.99%)
Monthly Payment: $300		Monthly Payment: $300
Payoff Period: 4yrs, 10 months		Payoff Period: 3yrs, 4 months

Total Interest Paid: $7240   **Total Interest Paid: $1987**

WOW! What a big difference! We're talking about a savings of $5,253!! And you'll be done paying off that credit card 1 year and 6 months sooner. So, as you can see, a five minute phone call is actually quite important. Agreed?

Now pull out your other credit card statements, gather the same interest rate information for each, and pick up that phone and call each company to negotiate a better rate. When you're finished, you should have lower rates on at least some of your cards. Congratulations! You're one step closer to getting out of debt.

Tip #2: Increase Your Monthly Payments

With a lower interest rate on your credit card, more of your money is being applied towards your loan versus interest every month and your balance should get smaller much sooner. Another helpful suggestion I can make is for you to actually <u>increase</u> your monthly payment. Sound impossible? We'll get into how to do that later in the book, if you don't see any way that you can do that today.

Tip #3: Make Payments More Often

Another suggestion is to make two or three payments a month instead of one. The way these credit card companies work can be quite complicated, but basically they use a calculating method called "compounding interest." Let's look at an example. If you have a debt of $10,000 and your interest rate is 18.99 percent you could be paying $200 to $400 a month toward interest. What I want you to do is start making <u>two</u> $200 payments each month instead of making one payment of $400. What's the difference, you ask? Well, because the interest is compounded daily on the balance for that day, the moment you make your first payment of $200 that month, the balance goes <u>down</u> and doesn't accrue (accumulate) as much interest throughout the rest of the month. By the time you've made your second payment in the same month, more money is applied towards the principle. This could save you hundreds if not thousands of dollars, depending on your balance. So you pay the same amount each month, just pay half of it earlier, so you're cutting your costs. Cool, huh?

Tip #4: Get Rid of the Problem

If you bought this book, then you either needed more information about how money works, you wanted to understand your American Dream, or you just liked looking at the pictures. Whatever the reason, there's a possibility that you have financial problems, or at least financial misunderstandings. Hopefully what I've explained so far clears up some of your confusions. But if you really want to get out of debt and achieve your American Dream, there's one thing you have to do.

If you were living in a house infested with termites, and the place was ready to collapse, what would you do? YOU WOULD ELIMINATE THE PROBLEM AND FIND SOME ANSWERS! This is probably going to be the hardest part of the book for you, but I'm going to have to ask you to do this. Because that spending is eating away at your American Dream, here's what you need to do:

Go get your credit cards and CUT THEM UP!

I know, I know, this seems outrageous. But if you haven't figured out by now that you have a serious problem with your spending, then you need a wake-up call. I don't care if you throw the credit cards in the garbage disposal, cut them into tiny pieces, or burn them. If you can't bring yourself to do that, then simply put them in a bowl of water and put the bowl in the freezer. FREEZE YOUR SPENDING! That way if you need them in an emergency you can defrost them, but they won't be easily accessible.

If you truly feel that you can't live without your credit cards, keep one, maybe two at the most, in a warmer environment. This way you have them in case of an emergency. However, having more than two is unnecessary and will only cause you more problems in the future.

Tip #5: Change Your Thinking

As you let go of that plastic crutch, you'll need a new way of thinking. It's a pretty simple, yet sometimes very challenging phrase to get used to using, but it works. And it's truly the route out of debt. Just repeat the following sentence:

PAPER, NOT PLASTIC!

PAPER, NOT PLASTIC!

PAPER, NOT PLASTIC!

PAPER, NOT PLASTIC!

PAPER, NOT PLASTIC!

PAPER, NOT PLASTIC!

PAPER, NOT PLASTIC!

Can you say it? Can you pay cash for it? Don't use the plastic! ATM cards, even though made of plastic, are "paper" because it's cash directly out of your bank account. So use *PAPER, NOT PLASTIC!* Make this your new mantra. These words are the key to your Financial Health and Prosperity.

CHAPTER 15

The Big Picture:

Expenses vs. Income

By now you've looked at your credit card debt, started to attack that problem, and gotten a better understanding of what you owe and how long it's going to take to pay it off. It's pretty enlightening, right? Okay, so let's get into the next step of really understanding what you're dealing with, by confronting your basic finances.

Since you don't have a credit card statement for these types of purchases, it's going to be a little harder to come up with all of the spending figures. If you use computer software such as Quicken, QuickBooks, or another product, it will make this next step easier. But you don't have to have it. If you monitor your spending by going online and finding out how much money you have in the moment, then go online and get your bank statement for the last 30 days and write down where your money goes. Also, if you use credit cards for basic expenses, those figures should be available. Just remember to be honest with yourself and fill out the information fully.

Expenses

Let's start by getting all of that information together. This will give you a good idea of what goes out every month from your household. Use it to help you fill out the "Basic Expenses Worksheet."

Note: You can also download the financial spreadsheet from my website at www.thedebtlady.com

In the "Yearly" column you should fill in expenses that come up once a year like Christmas, birthdays, and vehicle registration, so that you can allow for them in your budget. The "Monthly" expenses are for rent, credit card payments and basic bills. The "Weekly" expenses are for things like groceries, dining out and that happy hour every Friday night. **IMPORTANT:** Make sure that only one column is filled in per category.

Be as thorough as possible because this is what YOU spend. If you have a spouse or someone else in the house who contributes to these expenses, have them do this exercise with you. Even children should be involved if they spend money from the household, so they can see exactly what money goes out and how it has to do with them. Perhaps it'll help them realize why it's important to contribute to the chores around the house and do their part in exchange for the family expenses.

Notice that we've included a "New American Dream Budget" column because you're going to want to start setting aside money to achieve those new goals. You'll figure out what that amount is later in the book, so for now just leave that line blank.

Basic Expenses Worksheet

MORTGAGE/RENT	Yearly	Monthly	Weekly
Mortgage	$	$	$
Mortgage 2nd	$	$	$
Rent	$	$	$
Home/Renters Insurance	$	$	$
TOTAL MORTGAGE/RENT	$	$	$

CREDIT CARDS (CC)

	Yearly	Monthly	Weekly
Total of all CC minimum payments	$	$	$
Future Payments Toward CC	$	$	$
TOTAL CREDIT CARDS	$	$	$

AUTO

	Yearly	Monthly	Weekly
Auto Loan/Lease #1	$	$	$
Auto Loan/Lease #2	$	$	$
Auto Gas and Maintenance	$	$	$
Auto Insurance	$	$	$
TOTAL AUTO	$	$	$

EDUCATION

	Yearly	Monthly	Weekly
Education (Tuition, School Supplies)	$	$	$
Child Care	$	$	$
TOTAL EDUCATION	$	$	$

MEDICAL

	Yearly	Monthly	Weekly
Medical Care	$	$	$
Medical insurance	$	$	$
Vitamins	$	$	$
Chiropractors, Alternative Care	$	$	$
TOTAL MEDICAL	$	$	$

HOUSEHOLD ESSENTIALS   Yearly   Monthly   Weekly

	Yearly	Monthly	Weekly
Utilities (Electric, Gas, Water, Trash)	$	$	$
Telephone (Cell, Home, Etc.)	$	$	$
Cable/Satellite TV	$	$	$
Internet	$	$	$
Life Insurance	$	$	$
TOTAL HOUSEHOLD ESSENTIALS	$	$	$

HOUSEHOLD MISC   Yearly   Monthly   Weekly

	Yearly	Monthly	Weekly
Dining	$	$	$
Groceries	$	$	$
Coffee	$	$	$
Children's Lunches	$	$	$
Happy Hour	$	$	$
Entertainment/Movies	$	$	$
Gym Membership	$	$	$
Clothes/Shoes	$	$	$
Haircuts	$	$	$
Toiletries	$	$	$
Cigarettes	$	$	$
Animals (Food, Vet)	$	$	$
Household Items	$	$	$
Laundry/Dry Cleaning	$	$	$
Club membership	$	$	$
Gift/Contributions/Donations	$	$	$
Student Loans/Back Taxes	$	$	$
Child Support/Alimony	$	$	$

Other	$	$	$
TOTAL HOUSEHOLD MISC	$	$	$

NEW AMERICAN DREAM BUDGET

	Yearly	Monthly	Weekly
American Dream	$	$	$

SAVINGS

	Yearly	Monthly	Weekly
401K Plans	$	$	$
Savings	$	$	$
TOTAL SAVINGS	$	$	$

YEARLY EXPENSES

	Yearly	Monthly	Weekly
Christmas	$	$	$
Birthdays	$	$	$
Vehicle Registration	$	$	$
Vacations	$	$	$
Insurance? What type?	$	$	$
Other	$	$	$
TOTAL YEARLY EXPENSES	$	$	$

Once you've fully completed the worksheet, look it over carefully and make sure you haven't forgotten anything. The nice thing about this sheet is that you can change it at any time. Next, you'll total up ALL of the spending and then break it down into how much goes out per week.

Here's how it works: Add up the Yearly, Monthly and Weekly lines and get a total for each column.

	Yearly	Monthly	Weekly
OVERALL TOTAL	$	$	$

Take the "Overall Total" <u>Yearly</u> amount and write it below:

$

Then divide that number by 52 (the number of weeks in a year) and write it in the box below. That will give you the weekly amount needed for your yearly expenditure:

$ <u>**Weekly Number**</u>

Next take the "Overall Total" <u>Monthly</u> amount and write it below:

$

Then multiply that number by 12 months and put it here:

$

Now take the above number and divide it by 52 weeks:

$	Weekly Number

Take the "Overall Total" <u>Weekly</u> amount and write it one of the boxes below. Now, take the other two "Weekly numbers" you see above and write them in the other two boxes.

$	$	$

Add up all three weekly numbers and write down the total here:

$	Total Expenses

This number is the weekly amount that's needed for you to pay all of your bills and never put another penny on a credit card. For the yearly amounts, if you set aside money each week in a savings account, you won't be short of money or surprised when that yearly expense such as the car registration or Christmas rolls around. You'll actually have the money to <u>pay cash</u> for it. Remember that phrase? Let's say it out loud once again: **PAPER, NOT PLASTIC!**

Income

Okay, now that you know the <u>exact</u> amount of money that you need to have every week to pay all of your bills, I want you to write down the amount of money that you <u>make</u>, because we're going to look at the Big Picture: Expenses vs. Income. List <u>every</u> source of income that comes into your household. Do the same thing you did with your expenses and be thorough with it. Fill in the amounts in the Income Sources Worksheet. This will be your WEEKLY income. So if you make a check monthly, simply do what you did with the expenses and calculate so that you have your weekly income number.

Income Sources Worksheet

Weekly

WAGES	$
TIPS	$
UNEMPLOYMENT	$
CHILD SUPPORT	$
ALIMONY	$
BABY SITTING	$
INTEREST INCOME	$
GARAGE SALES	$
PAPER ROUTE	$
POKER WINNINGS	$
HORSE RACES	$
MISC	$
TOTAL INCOME	$

Take the "Total Income" and "Total Expenses" from the above worksheets and write them down below. Well done!

TOTAL INCOME	$
TOTAL EXPENSES	$

Next, we'll compare what's going out the door to what you're bringing in—Income vs. Expenses, on a weekly basis. Ready? Drum roll, please...

Subtract your total expenses from your total income. This is the amount of money that you have left over every week—or <u>don't</u> have left over every week—to handle your bills. Now write down the difference below:

DIFFERENCE	$

When you calculate everything you're spending versus bringing in, are you in the red or in the black? I mean, are you short of cash—in the red—or do you have money left over—in the black?

People have asked me why The Debt Lady character is always drawn in red and black. Here's why. In accounting, if you're "in the red," that's bad, because you've spent more than you had and your account is in the negative. But if you're "in the black," you're in the profit area and have money left over. Do you have money left over or are you short every week? Did you even finish filling it out!? If not, go back and do it now. I'll wait here. When you're ready, I'll show you how to tackle all that red and come out in the black, with a **PLAN.**

CHAPTER 16

<u>Honey, I Shrunk the Budget</u>

When you finally looked at the Big Picture of your Income vs. Expenses in that last chapter, did you notice yourself getting upset or worried? Well if you did, it's normal. Everybody has <u>some</u> type of reaction: they get mad, or they cry, or sometimes they just laugh hysterically. Typically it's because finances were something that they didn't know how to confront before. Now that they're confronting things, they realize that it's not as bad as they thought, because now they can <u>see</u> the big picture, which makes it more real and less scary in the long run.

If you found that you have money left over at the end of the week, that is, you're "in the black," then you need to set a goal to use that money to <u>pay off your credit cards</u>. Whether you have money left over at the end of the week or not, this next step is a **must** for <u>everybody</u> to *DO*, so that you can actually get out of debt as well as understand how to avoid getting back into it in the future.

<u>Find and Cut</u>

Since you've solved the mystery of where your money's gone, you can now dig even deeper and attack the problem, so your cash won't disappear so quickly from now on.

I want you to go back and look over your Total Expenses Worksheet, especially in the area of "Household Misc" because this is an area where you can tighten your belt. Look it over thoroughly and see what you can do without or do with <u>less</u>. Such as that weekly (or daily) after-work happy hour with friends, those 10 movie rentals per month, those 5 monthly magazines you never read anymore, or your weekly "mani-pedi" trip to the nail salon. Don't get me wrong, I love getting my nails done and I'm not telling you to stop. But in order to get these credit cards paid off, you're going to have to make some sacrifices. Besides, have you realized yet that the American Dream is NOT about having a bunch of stuff?

Let's continue our detective work and find more spending areas that can be cut back.

Are you spending more money eating out than you spend on groceries? If so, then you should think about packing your lunches and spending more time in the kitchen and less time at Taco Bell. Also, pay attention to those pesky expenses that you really don't need, like HBO and other movie and sports channels. If you just downsize your cable bill and your coffee/dining out bill, you can cut hundreds off of your expenses per month.

Even if you are in the black, you can still likely find several hundred dollars a month more if you cut back on a few things. **Find and cut, find and cut.** Remember the goal: to be out of debt and pay cash for everything.

You can start <u>right now</u> by picking up the phone and calling the cable company, or by talking to your family about eating out less. Once you're done cutting the wasted money, update the amounts listed on your Basic Expenses Worksheet. The beauty of this system is that <u>you</u> are in charge of your worksheet and <u>you can</u> decide what goes in or out. Feels good to finally be in control, doesn't it?

Now that you've cut down on your expenses and have even _more_ money every week to play with, I want you to go back to your Credit Card Debt Worksheet and find the credit card that has the _smallest balance_ due with the _highest interest rate_. This is the card that you'll be targeting to pay off first.

Take the amount of extra money per week that you now have because of your cut-backs in spending, and use that money to pay off this one credit card. Yep. You heard me right. You're going to take the money you saved by cutting expenses or that you have left over and apply that amount to this credit card every week, not every month. Obviously, you'll continue to make the minimum payments on this card, and apply the additional money that you have to it. Remember how I said you can cut your debt faster if you pay several times a month instead of once a month? Well, by making a weekly payment, you're paying that card off much faster, and not running up all that extra interest based on a higher balance. Here's where you *DO* that. Use the money you saved by cutting back on your weekly expenses, and PAY OFF THAT CREDIT CARD.

Remember to cut up the card you're paying off or put it in a bowl of water in the freezer so that you can't run up any more charges on it. This is the most important part. Make minimum payments <u>monthly</u> or spread out the monthly payment <u>weekly</u> on all of your <u>other</u> cards except the one that you are working on paying off. Make your <u>weekly</u> payment to that credit card religiously.

Once that account is paid in full, which should happen very quickly depending on the balance and the weekly payment, target your <u>next</u> credit card to pay off. Again, you should pick the one with the lowest balance but the highest interest rate. Next you're going to take the amount that you've been paying per week on the now paid-off credit card and apply that amount to this second targeted card, and send in that amount weekly. Same setup. You got it? Here's the step-by-step process:

Target-Freeze-Pay Off

1. TARGET a credit card with a low balance due and a high interest rate.

2. FREEZE all spending on it.

3. Take the money you've saved through your expenses cutbacks and send that extra cash in weekly to PAY OFF this credit card. Pay four times a month!

4. When that credit card is paid off, select the <u>next</u> card to target, freeze and pay off. ATTENTION! Every time you payoff a credit card, take yourself and your family out to a nice fancy dinner. Reward yourself! And remember, when you pay one off, move on to the next. But this time, pay a little bit more.

5. Adjust both your Credit Card Debt Worksheet and your Basic Expenses Worksheet as you accumulate more money from having these cards paid off.

6. Congratulate yourself with every payment you make! Good Job!

Learn While You Earn

Along the way other expenses will pop up, but you have to make choices as to what gets cut out of the expense budget in order to pay for each new item. For example, let's say the family wants a new 50 inch TV, and it costs $500. If you can cut eating out or some other expense by $50 per week, then you can put that money aside and in 10 weeks you'll have your TV. BUT DON'T BUY IT UNTIL YOU HAVE THE CASH TO PAY FOR IT.

Everybody in the family can pitch in and help donate to the "TV fund." That way they all contribute to what they want, and at the same time they learn the actual practice of budgeting, financial control, and creating cash vs. debt. They learn how to make conscious choices. All of you will feel better about this if you earn it as a group, so make it a game and see how much sooner you can get your TV if you all work together. Warning: Don't be swayed by those "On Sale Now!!!" advertisements. There will always be another sale—next week, next month—and by then you'll really save by paying cash when you have it!

Remember, the first step is to DECIDE that you want to *BE* in charge of your finances. Then once you've decided to *BE* that person, then *DO* your budget and *DO* it thoroughly. After it's done, keep it updated so that you know exactly what's going in and out of the household every week. This doesn't mean that you have all of your attention on your finances all of the time. It means that you know what you can spend and what you can't, and you're in control of your decisions and choices. Sit down at least once a week and pay your bills and keep track of where you're at financially. Make sure everybody in the family knows where you're at too.

There's no need to have your attention on finances everyday because if you're handling them once a week, and you know what you can spend on certain things, then you can concentrate on those other things in life that contribute to your American Dream. And by all means, MAKE MORE MONEY. It's the best advice I can give you. Instead of cutting and cutting and not having those things that you want, make more money and get them. But pay CASH! Live your life well and with those things that you want to *HAVE*, but buy them based on your ability to pay for them and not because some advertiser tells you to buy them, or because some bank says they'll give you a loan for them. If you have decided, while reading this book, to shoot for the *BE* that you always wanted and you have to go to school or get some training in order to reach that goal, keep your eyes on that American Dream. By making new choices, you'll get there faster. Ready to ramp it up? Here we go.

CHAPTER 17

<u>Your American Dream</u>
<u>Budget & Action Plan</u>

This may be even scarier than facing your credit card debt. Because now, I'm going to have you actually write down your American Dream and what it will take to achieve it. Keep breathing. Exhale. Okay. Let's go.

Pull out that list of your American Dream Goals, on page 149 and 150, and your Personal Worth Sheet on page 125 and 126. Now take each goal that YOU want, not what somebody else said you wanted, and list what you have to *DO* to make them happen. This is your Action Plan. The first thing I want you to do is write down all of those things that you can *DO* to obtain your dream that doesn't cost any money. Is it research, planning, talking to experts, checking into a certain industry, talking to your local Chamber of Commerce, making a new Facebook page, or calling your friends? Whatever it is, write it down, and remember, these don't cost you a cent to achieve. Put in things that you can *DO* every day to achieve that *BE* that you've always wanted. This includes a new job or career change; investigate what you need to *DO* to get what you want! Start writing!

As you can see, I've given you a lot of room to write this part because MONEY should never stop you from working toward your dreams. You can be *DOING* all of these things and spend nothing. Now, let's put an Action Plan together for things that do need to be purchased at some point to assist you in your process. Most things in life aren't free. We all know that, so don't expect to get everything you want for free. It's a nice concept but not too realistic. However, what I am trying to do is get you to realize that you don't *HAVE TO HAVE* (money) before you can *BE* or *DO*. *BE* and *DO* and the *HAVE* will come.

I've put a deadline date for each action, and a place for you to initial where you've completed that one task. First, figure out what it'll cost—that's your budget. Then take that number and put it into your Basic Expenses Worksheet under the "New American Dream Budget" category. That way you can start setting aside money to pay for your dream, while you're doing those things that you can *DO* that you don't have to pay for.

Look at the example below to get started:

AMERICAN DREAM ACTION PLAN (EXAMPLE)

GOAL: Working Actor

BUDGET

Acting Schools/Classes:	$900.00
Wardrobe (for headshots, auditions):	$250.00
Headshots by Professional Photographer:	$400.00
Resume & Headshots Printing:	$75.00
Mailing Lists (casting directors, agents, managers):	$60.00
Resume & Headshots Postage	
(mail to casting directors, agents, managers):	$82.00

**TOTAL COST: $1,767.00

Put this number into the **"New American Dream Budget Total" line of your Basic Expenses Worksheet and determine how much you're going to set aside weekly in order to get this done.

ACTION PLAN (EXAMPLE)

	DEADLINE	INITIAL
1. Research acting schools	05/30	*JYL*
2. Develop budget to pay for acting school	06/15	*JYL*
3. List actor prep expenses in worksheet	06/16	*JYL*
4. Develop actor resume	06/30	*JYL*
5. Research headshots, get headshots done	07/18	*JYL*
6. Print headshots & resume	08/30	*JYL*
7. Buy/find agents, directors mailing list	09/15	*JYL*
8. Mail headshots/resumes to list	09/28	*JYL*
9. Do follow-up calls, cards to list	10/15	*JYL*
10 Target acting class start date/cost	10/26	*JYL*
11. Start acting class	11/09	*JYL*

AMERICAN DREAM ACTION PLAN - SUMMARY

In summary the whole process is simple:

1. *DECIDE* who or what you want to *BE*.

2. *BE* that person by telling everybody that you are, especially yourself.

3. Put together a plan where you can *DO* things to *BE* that person without spending ANY money.

4. Put together a plan, if money is needed, and pay for those things to continue to *DO*.

5. Make target dates and stick to them.

6. *DO* something EVERYDAY toward your decision to *BE*.

7. Hit the targets you've set for yourself and sign them off.

8. Continue *DOING* until you *HAVE* what you're looking for. If it's that dream you've had since you were a child, a new profession, to own your own business or become a mechanic, whatever it is, this Action Plan can assist you to achieve it.

You could have 10 Action Plans going all at once because there are a lot of things that you want to *BE, DO*, and *HAVE*. So don't deprive yourself with one, reach for the stars and your full potential. If you don't know where to start I would recommend that you just pick one thing and do it. Then go to the next and then the next, and eventually all of your dreams will come true!

CHAPTER 18

Making More Money is Easier

I find it fascinating, and have seen it so many times, that when a person puts this whole "money/debt management" thing together, he starts making more money simply because he's doing what he intends to do by fulfilling his own purposes and goals. And more importantly, he understands and knows what it's going to take to get where he wants to go.

This is exactly what happens with finances. When someone has the full picture of what comes in and what goes out, then they can make new choices and take control of their lives. They now have the understanding that's needed to no longer have all of their attention on money. This ultimately frees up their attention to be able to do those other things in life that make them happy. As I have said so many times in this book, happiness does NOT come from having STUFF, it comes from *BEING, DOING* and *HAVING* those things that you *DECIDE* to *BE, DO* and *HAVE* without outside influences. In some cases it does have to do with having an item, like a new car. But in order to truly *have* that new car just follow these steps, and then having that car will be your reward to yourself, instead of being a problem or regret because you couldn't afford it.

Just picture it: No credit card debt, money to pay cash for everything you need, an extra $500-$5,000 or more per week in a savings account, a retirement account, a college fund for your kids, or for your new American Dream. Buy that fantastic house, car or whatever your heart desires! Now that's more like it! If you want to *HAVE* all that stuff, then by all means, *HAVE* it. Get that new car and house and make weekly payments, buy all those gadgets with cash and make tons of money. I want you to *HAVE* everything that you want in life, just *HAVE* them with honesty, integrity, understanding and *BEING* exactly who *YOU* want to *BE*.

Since the average credit card debt takes 47 years to pay off if you only make the minimum monthly payments, it's hard to imagine retirement or any rosy future. But with no credit card debt, the future is bright and the money has a tendency to flow freely in all directions! That's right. It's easier to make money when you have control of your finances, your decisions, and ultimately, your life. By doing the exercises I've listed in this book and making them a part of your life, you'll learn how to handle your finances, budget your money, and pay off your debt. What does this have to do with the American Dream? Everything! You're finally *BEING* that person who is confident and secure with themselves and in control of their future.

Now that you've gotten through this book, answer these questions for yourself:

- **Has my definition of the American Dream changed and if so, what is it now?**

- **Does my American Dream have everything to do with stuff or is it something more?**

- **Have I made any decisions?**

- **Has accepting outside influences become a thing of the past?**

- **Have I learned anything?**

Answer honestly. I hope you got something out of this book because that's why I wrote it, to help **YOU** realize **YOUR** full potential and to reach for the stars!

Thank you for coming with me on this journey. It means a lot to me to know that you're in control and can help yourself to flourish and prosper. Do so with fervor!

The Debt Lady says, "Pick up the napkin, put it in your lap and take control of your life."

About the Author

When I look back over the past 30 years it's interesting to see all of the curves in the road that got me where I am today. I didn't take the conventional route, the one that starts with a bachelor's degree in business and ends with an M.B.A. One could say that I attended the School of Hard Knocks. I learned what I know by experience, and I've been able to use that experience to help thousands of people manage their money, get out of debt, and regain control of their finances.

I'm a California girl, born and raised. But after a messy divorce in the early 80's I lost everything and moved out of state to regroup and get back on my feet. With my two baby girls in tow, I took a job as a bill collector for a collection agency. It was tough! I was dealing with my own financial drama and had to listen to others' troubles day after day. But it was the first of many lessons I would learn on the subject of credit.

There is a viewpoint prevalent among bill collectors that people are trying to get out of paying their debt. Since I was also one of those people, I knew that this wasn't necessarily true. People get themselves into financial trouble for all sorts of reasons. Sometimes it's lack of education, sometimes it's an unexpected illness, divorce, or countless other reasons. The bottom line is always the same: They can't pay, NOT they don't want to pay.

As you can imagine, over the next many years I'd heard it all from consumers, and then later from corporations who couldn't pay their debt. I managed to dig myself out of my own financial difficulties along the way, and started noticing that all was not well in the ever-changing lending industry. Collections had evolved from mostly hardship cases--people who had big hospital bills and no insurance, to people who'd over-extended themselves with credit cards. Lenders were going crazy, trying to lure consumers with the best deal, the best rate, the biggest credit limit. But what I began to notice was the lack of accountability on the part of lenders, and the apparent lack of understanding from consumers. How were people going to pay for all this stuff they were charging?

By 2002 I'd made my way back to California and had gotten out of the collection business altogether. I started working for a small debt settlement company in Los Angeles. Debt settlement was a relatively new concept, both to me and to consumers. But with my background and extensive experience in collections, it was a good fit for me to now help people handle the mess they'd gotten themselves into. I moved up the ranks of that company within a few short months, and became vice president of operations. I felt I'd found my calling--helping people with their financial difficulties.

In 2005 I started consulting on my own. That's about the time that I became known as "The Debt Lady." I made quite a name for myself, getting calls day and night from people and companies who'd heard that I could help them with debt settlement. I spent the next year flying all over the country answering people's questions and helping them figure out how best to handle their debt. I was spread too thin! So in 2006 I launched my first debt settlement company. I started it out of my living room with a handful of clients and one employee, and by the end of the year we'd moved into offices with over 2500 clients.

I've always had a tremendous desire to help people. Because of my experience, helping people with their finances seemed like a logical move. I've looked at this industry from both sides, seen the good and the bad, and can tell you that the only thing that remains the same is CHANGE. Over the years I've been able to help thousands navigate the often turbulent and ever-changing waters of the lending industry. Now I offer my years of experience and knowledge to you.

Jerri Simpson is "The Debt Lady"

Coming Soon!

The Debt Lady presents:

A series of easy-to-read booklets that help with every kind of financial situation you can think of. These booklets address:

Children and finances
Bill collectors and how to handle them
Lawsuits and Judgments
Loan Modifications
Credit Scores and credit repair
Real-estate

The list goes on and on. If you'd like to have more information about a specific topic, send me an email at thedebtlady@thedebtlady.com and give me your ideas! We can work on it together.

Follow me on Twitter, Facebook, Blogspot & Linkedin by visiting my website at: **www.thedebtlady.com**

www.ingramcontent.com/pod-product-compliance
Lightning Source LLC
Chambersburg PA
CBHW051451170526
45166CB00001B/206